Differentiated
Lessons
for Every Learner

Standards-Based Activities and Extensions for Middle School

Differentiated Lessons
for Every Learner

Dina Brulles, Ph.D.,
Karen L. Brown,
and Susan Winebrenner

PRUFROCK PRESS INC.
WACO, TEXAS

Library of Congress Cataloging-in-Publication Data

Names: Brulles, Dina, author. | Brown, Karen L., 1960- author. | Winebrenner,
   Susan, 1939- author.
Title: Differentiated lessons for every learner : standards-based activities
   and extensions for middle school / by Dina Brulles, Karen L. Brown, and
   Susan Winebrenner.
Description: Waco, Texas : Prufrock Press Inc., [2016] | Includes
   bibliographical references.
Identifiers: LCCN 2015049598| ISBN 9781618215420 (pbk.) | ISBN 9781618216113
   (epub)
Subjects: LCSH: Middle school education--Activity programs. | Middle
   schools--Curricula. | Individualized instruction.
Classification: LCC LB1623 .B745 2016 | DDC 373.236--dc23
LC record available at http://lccn.loc.gov/2015049598

Edited by Katy McDowall

Cover design by Raquel Trevino

ISBN-13: 978-1-61821-542-0

At the time of this book's publication, all facts and figures cited are the most current available. All telephone numbers, addresses, and website URLs are accurate and active. All publications, organizations, websites, and other resources exist as described in the book, and all have been verified. The author and Prufrock Press Inc. make no warranty or guarantee concerning the information and materials given out by organizations or content found at websites, and we are not responsible for any changes that occur after this book's publication. If you find an error, please contact Prufrock Press Inc.

Prufrock Press Inc.
P.O. Box 8813
Waco, TX 76714-8813
Phone: (800) 998-2208
Fax: (800) 240-0333
http://www.prufrock.com

Table of Contents

Chapter 6: Special Areas and Electives Extension Lessons

Music

Arts and Theatre

Physical Education

Foreign Language

Dedication

This book is dedicated to, and was inspired by, our amazing gifted teachers in Paradise Valley Unified School District and to the many teachers throughout the country who recognize the diverse ways in which students learn. Your students are fortunate to have you!

Acknowledgments

We would like to acknowledge and respect those of you who are seeking methods for ensuring all of our students are engaged in meaningful learning experiences. Your students deserve and appreciate your efforts.

Sincere gratitude goes out to all of the teachers who have contributed creative ideas for some of the lesson activities in this book. Special recognition goes to Becki West-Keur, whose brilliance and efforts influenced this work, especially in the special areas chapter. We are honored to have her teaching our gifted students in Paradise Valley. Lastly, we would like to thank our husbands, Dr. Mark Joraanstad, Daniel Brown, and Joe Ceccarelli, for their continued support of our work.

Foreword

When I began teaching in the early 1970s, I quickly became as bored with the learning activities in the curriculum as my students were. As a new teacher, it did not take me long to figure out that when I enriched the basic curriculum with extended thinking activities and provided opportunities for my students to choose from a list of assignments, they *all* became fully engaged in their learning. Even with my best efforts, however, it was difficult to create these opportunities with consistency across the school year. Several years later, I had the opportunity to take a course with Sandra Kaplan, Differentiating Curriculum for the Gifted Student. This course changed my approach to teaching forever. I now had a blueprint for differentiation—change the content, change the thinking processes, and/or change the products. I began to differentiate learning tasks for my middle school students by creating assignment menus in mathematics and language arts. This was not only an effective approach for gifted learners, but for all learners. And let's face it, gifted learners—those who have been identified for G/T programs and those who have not—all spend a good deal of time in the general education classroom.

I work now with teachers across the country to find more effective ways to get students to think deeply. The issue they struggle with most is finding the time and resources to develop and manage implementation of high-quality learning tasks that move students beyond "canned" answers to deeper thinking. Doing this within the required standards-based curriculum adds another layer of challenge for teachers. Deeper thinking takes time; students enter at different levels of readiness. Norman Webb's Framework of Depth of Knowledge (DOK) levels can fine-tune our understanding of how students "process" and engage with content and expand our concept of differentiation. Still, there have been few practical curricular resources that accurately interpret what DOK means and how to apply DOK levels across subject areas.

Finally there is a book that offers a plethora of high-quality options, closely aligned to the standards that teachers must teach. In *Differentiated Lessons for Every Learner*, Brulles, Brown, and Winebrenner prove that the marriage of DOK and differentiation for all students can result in using the required curriculum as a springboard for learning that is deeper and more meaningful for students. There is a lot to like—no, maybe love—about this book—in both philosophy and practicality. It is a needed book. It fills a void. I think it will be an important book for general education, special education, and gifted education teachers alike.

First of all, the learning activities in this book are designed with the student in mind. Multiple optional activities, aligned with clusters of standards, naturally emerge from what all students are currently learning. This approach allows for flexible groupings based on entry points for different students and varied teaching methods. It also encourages student choice and students taking the initiative to plan and sustain individual and group projects. Because deeper thinking is at the heart of the examples, I can envision the roles of teachers and students shifting from teacher-directed to more student-directed learning over time. These are not just fun activities; they are designed to engage students.

Secondly, this approach is based in what we know about best practices for instruction, assessment, and deeper learning. Preassessment and formative assessment practices are encouraged with guidance as to how to determine a good match for each student or groupings of students. Learning activities are not simply about the verbs used in descriptions, but the complexity of content and thinking expected as evidence in the final products. Many examples allow for meaningful collaboration, which we know from research is good for deeper thinking and learning.

Finally—and probably most importantly—this book is teacher friendly! Even someone who has had little prior exposure to DOK or differentiation can pick it up, skim a chapter related to what they currently teach, and begin to generalize ways it could be applied in their own classrooms. Grade-level or PLC teams can use it as a resource to develop common performance assessments of deeper thinking in each content area. And after so many years of the focus being mostly on mathematics and language arts, the door has been opened for teachers of all students and all subject areas to be at the table to develop common understandings of what rigor looks like. This is a book with the potential to bring new energy to the way we teach and envision how students learn.

—Karin Hess, Ed.D.
President, Educational Research in Action, LLC

Introduction

In this rapidly evolving era, innovative ideas abound and teachers have an abundance of tools at their fingertips. New technologies emerge every day, exponentially expanding the number of available resources. With this expansion, students have more choices in how they pursue and demonstrate their learning than ever before. This is an exciting time to be a teacher!

Methods that have been used for the instruction of gifted and talented students for decades are now being integrated into meaningful learning experiences for all students. The Common Core State Standards (CCSS; National Governors Association Center for Best Practices, & Council of Chief State School Officers [NGA &CCSSO], 2010a, 2010b) encourage the use of 21st-century skills, technology integration, and performance-based assessments. These learning experiences emphasize critical and creative thinking and can include integrated units of study. Within this context, there is renewed emphasis on appropriate pacing for students with atypical learning needs. Increasing rigor and challenge for advanced learners can expose all students to these possibilities. These higher expectations have the potential to lead to higher achievement for all, thus raising the bar for all students, regardless of grade level or content.

The time is upon teachers to implement interdisciplinary learning experiences that provide real-world connections and engage students in relevant and meaningful learning opportunities. The extension lessons in this book will help teachers incorporate interdisciplinary learning activities that provide rigor and challenge through content enrichment.

Teachers have long known that gifted students thrive when they have choices in their learning, even more so when their choices include open-ended learning activities that involve correlating and synthesizing information and using creative processes that encourage the production of original ideas. Isn't this what teachers want for all students? The reality in most classrooms is that there are some students who are ready for higher level of study in some areas, yet are at a more foundational level in other areas. There are also students who are working at a foundational level in all areas. For these students, teachers need to provide a self-reflective process for them to develop necessary skills and learn to think strategically. This will help students take ownership of their learning and strengthen their ability to self-direct.

Historically, the educational process has made students wait until they have the basics before they move on to more complex learning. However, we have seen many situations in which students are much more motivated when they are learning foundational skills in the context of more meaningful scenarios (e.g., when students are engaged in active learning such as building or cooking something, measuring for real-life applications, or solving or studying a real-life situation occurring in their school or community). Many students with learning difficulties also prefer more active learning experiences. Learning the necessary skills within meaningful contexts can provide more successful learning outcomes than experiences that keep these students in entry-level learning activities.

Teachers are expected to provide work at a challenge level for all students in large, mixed-ability classes, while also ensuring that the learning activities address the standards. Teachers need help preparing to teach in this differentiated instructional process. The extension lessons in this book demonstrate how to accomplish this daunting task through sample lessons that describe the process and are aligned to Depth of Knowledge (DOK) levels (Hess, 2013).

What Are Extension Lessons and How Were They Designed?

The extension lessons in this book are intended for use in almost any middle school classroom and were designed to address the ability levels of all students. The activities within each lesson were developed according to DOK levels, CCSS, and the national history (National Council for the Social Studies [NCSS], 2013) and science standards (NGSS Lead States, 2013). Each lesson states the specific standards addressed and lists the extension activities according to DOK level (a CCSS alignment chart is provided on the book's webpage at http://www.prufrock.com/assets/client pages/differentiated_lessons.aspx). The standards selected are representative of those addressed by the extension activities and are not all-inclusive. By utilizing DOK levels, teachers can guide students to activities that promote productive struggle with the topic of study. Each extension lesson contains learning activities at each DOK level, thus providing students with additional choice while working within their challenge range.

Why Is This Book Needed?

Content-area teachers are presented with the challenge of teaching not only the content-specific skills for their subject area, but also integrating language arts and literary skills. As teachers delve more deeply into the CCSS, it has become evident that simply writing an essay in biology class or reading a nonfiction article on a mathematician in advanced math class will not address the English language arts (ELA) rigor identified in the standards. The CSSS for English Language Arts & Literacy in History/Social Studies, Science, and Technical Subjects (NGA & CCSSO, 2010a) broaden teachers' thinking with regard to the skills and content to be integrated into specific subject areas. Teachers across the country wrestle with finding the time and resources to successfully tackle this challenge. This book provides one way to accomplish this feat by using activities designed to facilitate standards integration.

The CCSS for ELA necessitate that learning activities involve students' abilities to incorporate critical thinking, self-directed learning, collaboration, problem solving, and creativity. Doing so requires teachers to incorporate these constructs into daily lesson plans within each subject area. To incorporate the CCSS for ELA into specific curricular areas, teachers must identify the standards their lessons address. They then should address these standards at the varying levels of depth and complexity based on students' diverse learning needs. The extension activities included in this book facilitate that process.

Benefits of incorporating extension lessons into curriculum include:

 ➢ preparing students for performance-based assessments,
 ➢ providing instruction that is rigorous and relevant,
 ➢ emphasizing individual student accountability,
 ➢ documenting mastery levels beyond grade-level standards,
 ➢ encouraging flexible grouping of students for specific instructional objectives,
 ➢ providing for project-/problem-based learning,
 ➢ integrating technology into learning activities, and
 ➢ demonstrating enrichment that aligns to standards.

CCSS and High-Ability Learners

For decades, best practices in general education have evolved from gifted education. This is because educators must continually seek methods for challenging advanced students beyond the basics and into deeper levels of understanding. The move toward the CCSS reflects this practice on a grand scale, as the standards derive in large part from instructional practices and strategies educators have been using in gifted education for years. Teachers who attend our gifted education workshops often ask, "Aren't these strategies good for all students?" Our response is, "Of course they are!" The higher level thinking strategies in the CCSS benefit all students.

Instruction for high-ability learners focuses on interdisciplinary concepts, critical thinking skills, and problem solving across domains and relative to standards. With the implementation of the CCSS, teachers continue to differentiate for gifted learners within a set of standards that are reasonably rigorous in each subject. Teachers understand the importance of continuing to accommodate the needs of gifted learners and providing the additional rigor and challenge students need to advance in their learning, while still teaching to the standards.

Standards do not define:

➢ how teachers should teach,

➢ all that can or should be taught,

➢ the nature of advanced work beyond the grade-level standard,

➢ the interventions needed for student success,

➢ everything needed to ensure college and career readiness, or

➢ a curriculum.

Although students who are radically advanced in certain areas may need opportunities to work with standards assigned to higher grade levels, the extension lessons in this book encourage teachers to move beyond solely accelerating standards. The lessons allow for learning beyond grade level while still embedding enrichment and critical thinking throughout all the content areas. This process occurs by incorporating open-ended opportunities to meet the standards through multiple pathways, more complex thinking applications, and real-world problem-solving contexts.

New types of assessments are helping to drive the instructional process. Students are now being assessed through performance-based activities and portfolio-style techniques, which are based on higher level learning outcomes. The instructional methods utilized throughout these lessons helps prepare students for the new types of assessments.

Teachers in all subjects are responsible for the CCSS for ELA content standards. Many wonder how to incorporate these standards in their domains and how to document that they are being addressed. The extension lessons specifically address these two challenges. The structure helps teachers document student progress throughout each extension lesson. The sample rubric design, along with directions for how teachers and/or students can use and create them, provides additional methods for documenting the standards addressed within each activity (see appendix).

Correlation With DOK Levels

We have identified the DOK level for each activity in every extension lesson. This delineation helps teachers easily identify the levels of activities to direct students to after completing formative assessments. Sometimes teachers will want to group students based on pretest results, and sometimes students will determine the level upon which to begin. Regardless of the method used, it is helpful for both teachers and students to clearly see the progression of complexity within each lesson.

The progression of complexity within the DOK levels build students' awareness of their learning needs. Self-reflection is invaluable in students' learning processes, as they work toward understanding how to direct their own learning. Providing students opportunities to reflect on their thinking on a daily basis fosters self-regulation and can deepen their understanding of the content being addressed.

In Chapter 1, we will discuss methods for determining students' groupings for assigning them to the various levels of activities within each lesson. Teachers will also learn how to develop and build on the skills students need to progress through the more complexly leveled activities. Lastly, teachers will be guided through the process of using and developing similarly tiered lessons in each content area.

The DOK-leveled learning activities require that students use critical and creative thinking strategies, especially in the activities found in the DOK 2, 3, and 4 levels. The levels of activities within each extension lesson are presented in a progression of complexity. Exposure to the higher level activities encourages students to consider and prepare for the next level of challenge, which sets the stage for additional rigor.

The Importance of Rigor

Rigor is the goal of helping students develop the capacity to understand content that is complex, ambiguous, provocative, and personally or emotionally challenging. (Strong, Silver, & Perini, 2001, p. 7)

Current educational trends are dispelling long-held misconceptions regarding teaching with rigor. Rigor does not come from the standards and skills to be taught, but rather in how the standards and skills are addressed with individual students. Rigorous instruction involves creating models in which students represent their findings and explore how their discoveries can make a positive difference in the world. This requires intentionally teaching the strategies students need to study challenging texts, detect bias, gather relevant information, and decide how to frame what they've learned in a useful way.

Rigor involves:

➣ learning strategies more than answers,
➣ understanding how to ask the right kinds of questions,
➣ thinking creatively and with agility,
➣ exploring the complex nature of the content,
➣ consciously including thinking skills in daily activities,
➣ exploring project-based activities,
➣ connecting to the world of the student,
➣ digging deeply into content,
➣ bringing adaptable skills to real-world situations,
➣ being able to communicate and collaborate on challenging projects, and
➣ accessing, analyzing, and evaluating information.

Rigor does not involve:

➣ completing 50 math problems for homework when fewer will demonstrate mastery,
➣ assigning additional worksheets to students who complete assignments quickly,
➣ simply using an honors textbook with your high-performing students, or
➣ covering more material in a shorter period of time.

The extension lessons in this book utilize DOK levels to provide rigor in a number of ways. The format allows all students to go deeply into content and explore the complex nature of that content. The majority of the lessons are project-based or problem-based and connect to real-world activities. They require students to rely on thinking skills. This process requires teachers to teach strategies rather than simply having students seek specific answers.

How This Book Fits With RtI

Response to Intervention (RtI) is a process for achieving higher levels of academic and behavioral success for all students through high quality instructional practice, continuous review of student progress, and collaboration (see Figures 0.1 and 0.2). As such, RtI has implications for all students including those in general education, special education, gifted and talented, Title I schools, English language learners (ELL), etc. Regardless of the student population, the RtI process is the same. The process embraces a rigorous core curriculum that is differentiated to respond to individual differences. The process employs increasingly intense interventions as needed by the students, which requires continuously reviewing students' progress.

In Chapter 1, we will discuss methods for creating lessons with activities that specifically address students' learning at all levels: Tier I, those needing the extra challenge of Tier II, and also the intense interventions needed by students in Tier III. Informal assessment strategies that inform teachers of where students fall on the RtI spectrum will also be shared in Chapter 1 and demonstrated in Chapters 2–6.

In *Beyond Gifted Education: Designing and Implementing Advanced Academic Programs* (2014), Peters, Matthews, McBee, and McCoach described the RtI process around the understanding that not all students have the same needs. The intervention each student requires is determined by measured need. This determination relies on achievement data. In the sample lessons (see Chapters 2–6) we share strategies for preassessment in the classroom. With this formative assessment data, teachers can consider flexible grouping configurations and determine the appropriate interventions the different groups need. Grouping advanced learners together and assigning more complex learning activities within a heterogeneous classroom provides a Tier II intervention within the class.

Highly complex learning tasks for those few students needing a Tier III intervention are included in every extension lesson. These DOK Level 4 learning activities require that students research, analyze, and correlate data from various sources, synthesize information, and bring forth novel ideas and unique perspectives. To succeed in completing open-ended and student-driven tasks at this level, students must learn to self-regulate and self-reflect on their learning processes.

Chrystyna Mursky from the Wisconsin Department of Public Instruction identified how several best practices in gifted education fit into the RtI framework (Rollins, Mursky, Shah-Coltrane, & Johnsen, 2009). As Tier II interventions, these strategies and methods allow for the appropriate level of challenge needed by most gifted students. How do you know if Tier II activities are sufficiently challenging for students or if they need Tier III interventions? This question can sometimes be answered through preassessment data, sometimes evidenced through student work, and sometimes determined or influenced by student motivation.

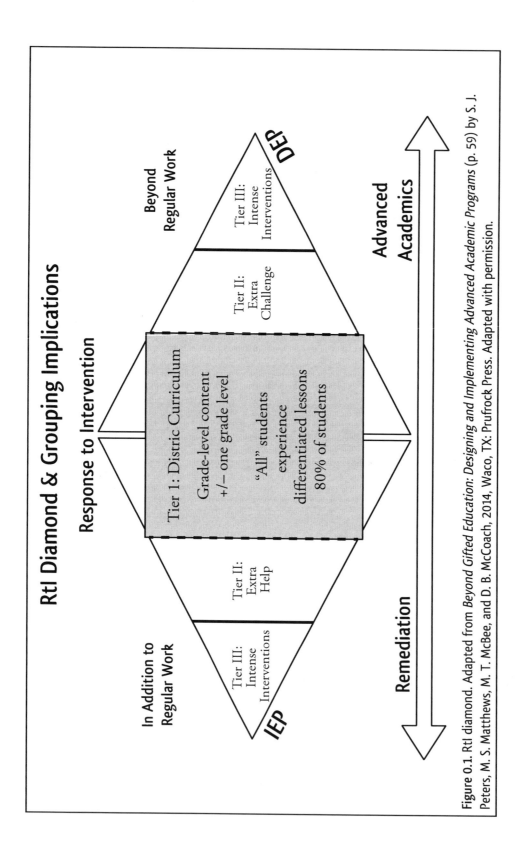

Figure 0.1. RtI diamond. Adapted from *Beyond Gifted Education: Designing and Implementing Advanced Academic Programs* (p. 59) by S. J. Peters, M. S. Matthews, M. T. McBee, and D. B. McCoach, 2014, Waco, TX: Prufrock Press. Adapted with permission.

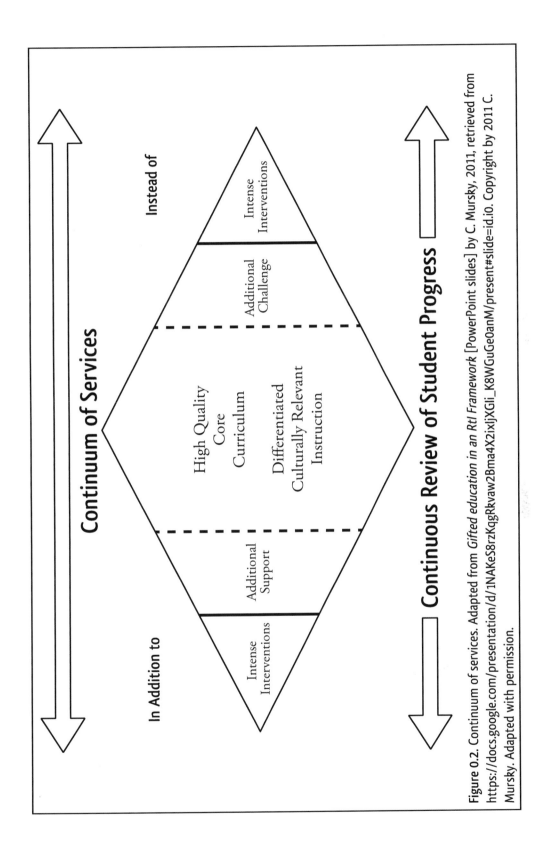

Figure 0.2. Continuum of services. Adapted from *Gifted education in an RtI Framework* [PowerPoint slides] by C. Mursky, 2011, retrieved from https://docs.google.com/presentation/d/1NAKeS8rzKqgRkvaw2Bma4X2ixIjXGii_K8WGuGe0anM/present#slide=id.i0. Copyright by 2011 C. Mursky. Adapted with permission.

Most teachers teach to Tier I most of the time with grade-level curriculum because this is where the majority of students begin. Teachers need guidance, not only in *how* to implement the Tier II and III interventions, but also in understanding *why* they are critically needed for high-ability students. Building that understanding and awareness into the mechanics of lesson design and delivery is critical. In this way, teachers learn to refine their instructional planning and implementation with high-ability students' needs in mind.

Classroom-based practices for gifted education within an RtI framework are detailed in Figure 0.3.

The interventions can be effectively implemented in a mixed-ability classroom. These strategies may also be used as Tier III interventions when other factors are included, such as mentoring, apprenticeships, radical acceleration, online curriculum, and other supports. The instructional design of the extension lessons embeds these classroom-based practices and strategies. These practices will be explained further in Chapter 1 and modeled in Chapters 2–6.

The sample lessons in Chapters 2–6 demonstrate the full process of planning and providing instruction that targets students' needs, as defined within the RtI framework. This process begins with pretesting to obtain the evidence needed for forming flexible learning groups. Rollins et al. (2009) further described the process teachers can follow within the RtI framework:

1. Establish relevant goals based on content standards, course or program objectives, learning outcomes, etc.
2. Specify the enduring understandings, or the big ideas, that are embedded in the goals, i.e., change, patterns, and power. Phrase the goals in ways that are relevant to students' experiences and interests in order to engage them in learning. This step focuses the curriculum on the profound ideas of the discipline, moving beyond, facts and information.
3. Develop essential questions that foster inquiry, understanding of the big ideas, problem solving, and transfer of learning.
4. Define what students will know and be able to do and how the knowledge and skills will help students master the enduring understandings. (p. 24)

Within the context of the extension lessons, Steps 1 and 4 address the planning, development, and assessment of the learning activities. Steps 2 and 3 are accomplished through the DOK-leveled learning activities. As Rollins et al. (2009) wrote:

According to McTighe (2008), the next step is determining what evidence will be gathered so that students can demonstrate that they have mastered the targeted knowledge, skills, and understandings. This evidence is composed primarily of authentic, complex performance tasks that provide students opportunities to grapple with ideas and issues. (p. 24)

Continuum of Services
for Students With Gifts and Talents

Frequently Used Interventions			
Classroom-Based	◆ Preassessment ◆ Questioning Techniques ◆ Creative Thinking ◆ Critical Thinking ◆ Flexible Grouping	◆ Problem-Based Learning ◆ Inquiry Models	◆ Curriculum Compacting ◆ Independent Contractors
School-/District-Based	◆ Cluster Grouping	◆ Pull-Out/Pull-In ◆ Purchased Services	◆ Subject Acceleration ◆ Grade Acceleration ◆ Mentorships ◆ Internships

Increasing Intensity →

Figure 0.3. Continuum of services for students with gifts and talents. Adapted from *Gifted Education in an RtI Framework* [PowerPoint slides] by C. Mursky, 2011, retrieved from https://docs.google.com/presentation/d/1NAKeS8rzKqgRkvaw2Bma4X2ixljX Gli_K8WGuGe0anM/present#slide=id.i0. Copyright 2011 by C. Mursky. Adapted with permission.

The activities in the extension lessons are designed to develop students' abilities to accomplish these complex tasks and processes. The lessons support "a focus on real-world contexts, ask students to apply knowledge and skills they have acquired to novel situation, and require students to support their work" (Rollins et al., 2009, p. 24).

Preparing for Performance-Based Assessments

The shift away from criterion and norm-referenced assessments leaves many teachers wondering how to prepare their students for assessment. The extension activities support that transformative practice. Within most of the activities, students are asked to create and develop understanding, and then defend their approach. This process prepares students for performance-based assessments. Working through the process of supporting understandings with textual evidence represents one means of preparing students for performance-based tasks. For students to be successful with a performance-based assessment format they must experience these situations on a consistent basis during the regular learning process. Use of extension lessons affords students the opportunity to develop and refine the skills needed for this type of assessment.

How This Book Fits With PLCs

Professional learning communities (PLCs) are established and run in a wide range of formats. In most cases, school administrators develop the framework. The PLC process is then driven by the school's goals and initiatives. Teachers meet regularly in PLCs to examine student data, determine desired interventions, and collaborate on plans for how they will move students forward. After studying student data, teachers have clear evidence that "moving forward" is going to look different for different students.

Although all students need to learn related content, data show that students need to study the content at different levels of complexity. The extension lessons provide concrete examples for how teachers can address and manage those different levels of learning. The discussions during PLC meetings help teachers group students by different challenge levels. Teachers determine the groupings by analyzing their data, which then allows them to plan for these different learning levels.

At each PLC meeting, teachers revisit the results of the lessons and their assessments planned in the previous meeting. Between meetings, teachers record student data—both grades and observations—and progress toward the identified goal. They use this data as both formative and summative assessments, which measure progress and suggest readiness levels that can indicate students' challenge levels—a critical step in the instructional planning process. Using extension lessons while planning in PLCs can also provide evidence of out-of-level learning and documentation of progress.

Real-World Application

Students enjoy learning that is relevant to their world. Many students hold deep interests in real-world events or have a passion for learning about certain topics. Many also bring a wealth of background knowledge to the classroom. Teachers can capitalize on these knowledge bases and areas of passion by providing students with open-ended learning opportunities that further develop their interests.

Many students thrive on the ability to follow ideas as they emerge. They get motivated by a challenge, become immersed in what they are learning, and retain more of what they learn when they can direct their own learning. Activities in the extension lessons, specifically those in the DOK Levels 3 and 4, present opportunities for students to pursue deeper meaning and make more complex connections within the specific topics being studied by in the class.

Students benefit from enrichment related to the content being studied. Enrichment, or learning activities that allow students to go above and beyond the regular curriculum, is an inherent aspect of the extension lessons. Enrichment is particularly important for students of high ability because of their propensity for completing grade-level work quickly and easily. In fact, they can often demonstrate mastery of content far beyond the level of the rest of the class before or while instruction occurs.

Enrichment activities, which allow students to apply their knowledge to real-world situations, add authenticity to their work. Planning is essential in this process. Incorporating or creating extension activities when developing unit lessons helps to ensure you will have the challenging activities available for students when needed.

Using This Book

This book includes:
- extension lessons tied to national standards and DOK levels,
- sample lessons and strategies on how to create your own,
- a rubric and basic forms that will help students keep records of their activities and progress (see appendix),
- suggestions of how to use the materials provided, and
- recommendations for ongoing meetings of interested teachers for the purpose of revising existing lessons or developing new ones.

Additional resources are available on the book's webpage at http://www.prufrock.com/assets/clientpages/differentiated_lessons.aspx.

Using the Extension Lessons

Teaching and learning in today's classrooms offers myriad possibilities, but with new, innovative instructional opportunities come new expectations. With the advent of the CCSS, performance-based assessments, and ubiquitous technology, teachers are learning new instructional approaches and students are experiencing new methods of learning. Middle school teachers are facing additional expectations, with the need to embed ELA instruction into their content areas. This book was written specifically to help middle school teachers integrate the content areas they teach with the CCSS for ELA while also embedding innovative learning approaches that build 21st-century skills.

The extension lessons expand upon regular grade-level learning activities and assignments. They offer project-based learning opportunities that drive students to think at deeper levels. The DOK-leveled lesson format provides varied levels of complexity, allowing students to work on the same topic while completing challenging learning activities based on their knowledge of the content and the complexity of their thought processes.

The methods for differentiating curriculum and instruction for gifted students discussed here could be viewed as overarching practices to use with all students. These methods apply to all the content areas. When working on these learning activities, students can delve deeply into content and explore areas of interest while also providing documentation of mastering the standards.

We recommend using extension lessons for most units of study. Students can work on the activities at different times and in different ways. Given that the activities are tiered to DOK levels, all students are able to work on the extension lessons. When adopting a tiered system such as this, each student can have an extension folder that is kept in a convenient location in the classroom. Students can retrieve their folders to work on extension activities at any time.

The extension lessons are designed to help teachers present content at the conceptual level for all students, which makes it easier to modify for high-ability students. With each extension lesson, teachers can integrate basic skills and higher order thinking skills. The extension lessons contain open-ended tasks that allow for in-depth learning based on students' interests and emphasize creative and productive thinking, while also ensuring adherence to standards. In this section, we provide suggestions on how to teach the research skills and self-evaluation strategies that students need when working on self-directed learning activities.

Teachers can use the extension lessons to further instruction in the following ways:

➤ after students demonstrate mastery through a pretest or other formative assessment,
➤ after students compact out of the regular assignment,
➤ as a regular part of their weekly instruction provided to all students in the class,
➤ to gauge and monitor students' ability to self-direct and set goals, or
➤ to build self-reflection skills as the students monitor progress toward their goals.

Teachers can also use them as substitute teacher plans. In this way, students can continue working on extension activities previously begun or can select a new one within the same topic if they are not currently working on one.

What Are the Benefits?

Developed by Dr. Joseph Renzulli, "curriculum compacting" means that students spend less time working on curriculum they have mastered or can master in a shorter amount of time than expected (Reis & Renzulli, 1992).

Using the extension lessons as a regular part of instruction provides students with continual opportunities to individualize their learning while everyone in the class studies the same content. The differentiated learning activities allow students to do the following:

➤ work at their challenge levels,
➤ pursue areas of interest related to the content being studied,

> ➤ research topics of interest,
> ➤ delve deeply into a topic,
> ➤ direct their own learning,
> ➤ activate prior knowledge,
> ➤ integrate multiple methods of learning,
> ➤ make connections to related content,
> ➤ draw upon previously learned content,
> ➤ create projects that demonstrate and document their learning,
> ➤ improve presentation skills, and
> ➤ set goals and monitor learning progress.

Teachers who have routinely used extension lessons feel they are providing differentiated learning opportunities to every student who needs them. Teachers find that the extension activities spark new and novel ideas that the students get excited about pursuing (Reis & Renzulli, 1992). No more feeling guilty that there are students sitting in class who are not benefiting from the general instruction!

Using the Lessons "As-Is" or Modifying the Lessons

The extension lessons can be used as is or with modification. This includes both generic plans, such as Lesson 2.6: Persuasive Writing (p. 47) and some more specific plans, such as Lesson 3.11: John Smith and the 13 Colonies (p. 90) and Lesson 5.2: Cell Structure (p. 151). You can modify activities by changing some of the elements. By changing a few words you can make the activities simpler or more complex. This can include adding or eliminating steps and making the activities more concrete or abstract.

At times you may want to modify a lesson's activities more significantly, and this can be done in a number of ways. The learning activities in some of the extension lessons can serve as models to use with different topics of study. For example, Lesson 2.17: *Chasing Vermeer* (p. 60) represents activities that pertain specifically to that book. However, teachers can modify the activities for a different book following a similar pattern. Many activities include general terms such as, "Cite several cases where . . . ." and "Provide examples of . . . . " Teachers may decide to specify quantities of examples or items within some activities, most frequently with activities of DOK Levels 1 and 2. You will find less need to quantify activities at the DOK Levels 3 and 4 due to the complex nature of the activities.

Getting Students Started

Students who are not accustomed to working independently will need guidance when beginning to work on extension activities. They will need direct instruction on their roles, responsibilities and procedures, and working conditions clearly defined and posted. Once these systems are in place they will become routine practices for students.

Because of the inherent variability of activities within the lessons, the approaches students take to complete the tasks will vary widely. To help students get started, teach them these steps:

> ➤ identify the objective,
> ➤ begin researching and accumulating data on the topic, and
> ➤ determine the project format in which to present the information.

Consider the sample lesson activity below and how Eli approached the activity.

Sample Lesson: Explorers of the New World

Activity: Create a "cause and effect" presentation of the impact the explorers had on the Native American civilizations in the New World (DOK 2).

First, Eli read through the standards included on the extension lesson and read the description of the activity. He then began researching explorers involved in exploration of the New World. He decided that in order to understand the impact the explorers had he needed to understand the Native American cultures prior to their arrival. He made note of those explorers who he thought "did good things for the Native American populations they encountered" and those who did not. Eli identified one explorer from each nation that interested him the most. Next, he made lists of their impact on the cultures they encountered. He then identified the cause/effect relationships. Eli identified events that transpired during their reign and the impact those deeds/events had on the empire.

With this information he created a digital presentation. His presentation included slides on each of the explorers that he researched, as well as on the Native American cultures with whom they interacted. He identified major themes within the explorers' actions and then created slides that compared and contrasted the individuals and the impact they had on the Native Americans in light of those themes.

How to Manage Extension Lessons

The extension lesson activities allow for sustained learning challenges. Most are not designed to be completed in a single day but rather to allow students to explore and extend learning over multiple days. The activities are student driven. The amount of time spent studying the extension activity is determined by the student and by the teacher's instructional plans. This means that students may routinely move back and forth between whole-group instruction and independent study. It is imperative that some form of pretesting takes place to determine where the students' knowledge levels lie in order to identify the appropriate level of challenge.

Sometimes, particularly in mathematics, the extension activities can be used for students who can demonstrate mastery through a pretest prior to receiving instruction on the material. When the content is new to the rest of the class, it may be that only those who have tested out will be working on the extension lessons. These students will then be able to study similar or related content, in deeper and more complex ways. The following situations in Mrs. Sharma's biology class present three different scenarios in which the extensions are commonly used.

Situation 1

Mrs. Sharma is introducing a unit on cell structure. Dani, whose parents are both physicians, has spent a considerable amount of time in labs and at home researching and learning various areas of biology. Her parents have been fostering this interest since she was a young child. Dani engages Mrs. Sharma in a deep discussion on the topic. Mrs. Sharma allows Dani to review the content she will be teaching and then take the end of the unit test. She obtained a very high score on the pretest and was then able to select a learning activity from a extension lesson Mrs. Sharma provided to her. The extension activity she selected was to investigate future possibilities of using Hirano bodies to prevent or treat disease.

Activity: Hirano bodies are important but poorly understood cell structures. Scientists hope they may eventually provide important information on the prevention and or treatment of some mysterious diseases, such as Alzheimer's, Lou Gehrig's disease, and others. Research this topic and decide if you feel it offers true hope to people who suffer from these and similar diseases. Support your findings in a pro/con format (DOK 4).

Dani and Mrs. Sharma create a plan in which Dani will document her daily progress toward her goal while working independently (see Daily Log of Extension Work, p. 245). Dani meets with Mrs. Sharma at regularly scheduled times for guidance and oversight. Dani completes her work on a Google doc that she has shared with her teacher. This way, Mrs. Sharma can view her progress and answer questions Dani posts on the doc.

Situation 2

During the unit, Mrs. Sharma also recognized that several students are catching on very quickly and easily completing assignments. She decides that these five students still need direct instruction to learn the content, but they require significantly less time than others to complete the work. She meets with the group and explains that she is going to compact the assignments so that they do not have to spend an excessive amount of time working on material that comes easily to them. Mrs. Sharma assigns them only the most difficult items. Upon completing these items, she then helps each student select an extension activity to work on. These students chose extension lessons in DOK levels 2 and 3.

Activities:
o Research several famous incidents of multiple births involving four or more babies. Demonstrate how unusual cell division leads to such events. Create a presentation in which you explain the relationship of the chemistry of fertility drugs to the events of multiple births (DOK 2).

o Study the thalidomide event of the 1950s. Find other examples of how a drug designed for benefit caused harm. Investigate the use of thalidomide today for symptoms other than the ones for which it was originally intended. Identify methods/procedures scientists use followed this time period to prevent similar events from happening in the future (DOK 3).

Situation 3

On Friday, Mrs. Sharma has all of her students working on extension lessons for a specified period of time. The extension lesson Mrs. Sharma availed to her class contains learning activities that can appropriately challenge all students, including those with emerging skills or learning challenges. All students work on their selected activities during this period. Because the menus contain eight choices of activities, there are some students working on the same activities. Mrs. Sharma allows students to work collaboratively on their activities during this time if they so desire.

In each of these scenarios, all of Mrs. Sharma's students are working at their individual challenge levels. In Situation 1, Dani clearly did not need additional instruction or practice on the material; however, she found great challenge in the DOK Level 4 activity she worked on during the instructional period. In Situation 2, the students who compacted out of the material by successfully completing the assigned work were able to enhance their study of the same content, but at more complex levels working on the DOK Level 2 and 3 activities. In Situation 3, all students were working on extension lessons at DOK Levels 1–4. Mrs. Sharma moves throughout the class during these times meeting with small groups, pairs, or individuals to facilitate their learning.

In Situation 2, which is the most common, students who begin working on a extension lesson on Day 1 of instruction would still participate in the whole-group instruction on Day 2 if the topic or material is new. Students who demonstrated mastery of the Day 2 materials would then able to continue working on their chosen extension activity. However, some of these five students might require additional practice on some topics and thus not move to an extension lesson until a later time. To know who is ready to work on the extension lessons, Mrs. Sharma routinely offers informal pretests and keeps this documentation for her records.

In Situation 3, the teacher has all students working on extension lessons as part of the regular instruction. This practice helps build community and collaboration within the class and presents access to critical thinking and problem-solving opportunities to all students. The students appreciate this time to work on activities of their choosing.

In regular mixed-ability classes, or where gifted students are cluster grouped, the teacher may create a system of continual pretesting to move students in and out of flexible groups where those who compact out of the regular curriculum work on extension lessons. This process can also occur in honors classes or self-contained gifted program classes. However, in classes with a majority of gifted and talented students, the consistent use of extension lessons can serve as regular practice.

In some situations, the teacher pretests and assigns a limited choice of extension activities to some students. In other situations, she discusses the options with a student and guides the selection. Sometimes she allows students to self-select. Given this variability, you may wonder:

> *What happens when students select activities that are beneath their challenge level?* In these cases, we recommend allowing the student to complete that activity, which should not take very long. When finished, instruct the student to select another activity. Students soon realize they are doing more work or "busy work" and usually begin selecting more challenging activities as their first choice. If they do not select challenging activities, the alternative is for them to go back to work with the class on material they already know and lose the opportunity to work on the extension lesson. They quickly learn the benefit of working on appropriately challenging activities and documenting their progress.

> *What happens when students complete their extension lesson while the class is working on related material?* Review the students' projects to see if additional work is needed. Have students then prepare for their presentations, present them to the class, take feedback, and complete self-evaluations. If time permits, students can select another lesson activity to begin.

> *What happens when students do not engage in the learning activity?* Students who do not follow the guidelines for independent work must go back to the regular instruction and work on the content in which they have already demonstrated mastery. This usually occurs just once, as students usually begin reflecting on their role and responsibilities when working independently on extension work.

Opportunities to Extend and Explore

Extension activities offer students opportunities to extend and explore topics in varied ways, deepening and enhancing understanding. Note that although all of the concepts within the extension lesson will be addressed at some level, some will not be explicitly taught. Direct instruction relates to the standard, topic, or lesson being studied. The peripheral and extended content related to the activities in extension lessons are pursued by the students working on those activities.

This approach provides students with productive struggle, a critical learning component. The goal is not to frustrate the students, but to provide them opportunities to struggle with the content as part of the learning process. Students need to learn how to persevere in the learning process when presented with a challenge. The level of independence inherent in this structure requires that students develop self-management skills and metacognitive abilities. With most students, these skills must be taught. Teachers can help students attain these skills through self-reflective processes.

As educators, our goal is to support students in the learning process. With this goal in mind, it is imperative that students have opportunities to participate in activities that promote all three dimensions of the learning process: acquisition, use, and extension. By connecting DOK levels to specific types of learning activities, teachers can readily direct students to the appropriate level of complexity (see Figure 1.1). Students will spend varying amounts of times working in the different DOK levels. The high-leveled activities that the academically advanced students select for study will naturally assume mastery of the lower level skills and content; these become embedded into the more challenging projects.

Creating Extension Lessons

The extension lessons in this book incorporate tasks that require a higher degree of student independence. The open-ended nature of many of the activities results in a wide range of projects produced by students. This is particularly true with lesson activities at DOK Levels 3 and 4. Students working at these levels enjoy pursuing their own ideas in the learning processes. These students need less structure because they will have already mastered the basics. Examples of how to gauge and document the level of independence needed are discussed below.

Students often have excellent ideas about how to pursue and demonstrate their understandings. You will find that at times they may want to modify the activities in some lessons. Recognize that students are using higher order thinking skills when they modify the lesson activities. Given the opportunity to develop their own activity in a extension lesson, or direct the process within an activity, student buy-in increases significantly. This is when truly meaningful learning begins.

When allowing students to modify or create extension activities, attempt to ensure that the level of rigor matches their levels of challenge. This begins by having a discussion with the student(s) regarding the standards and objective(s) to be addressed.

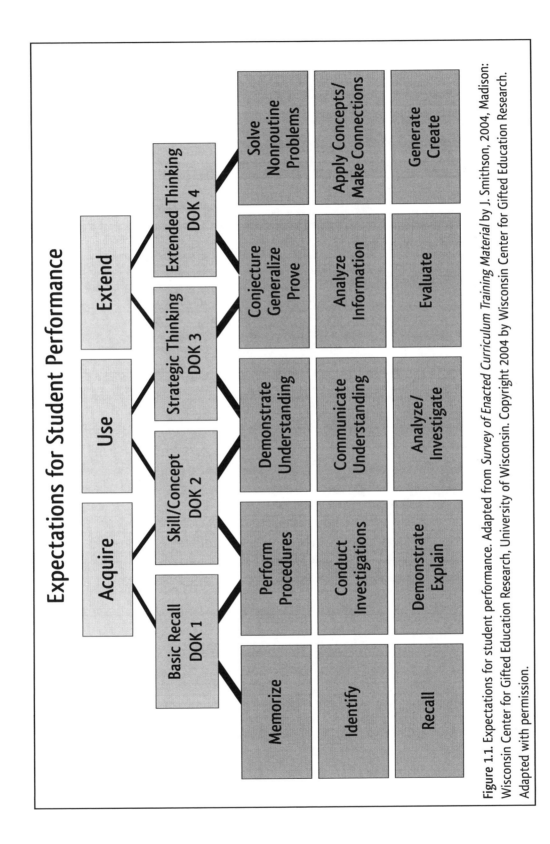

Figure 1.1. Expectations for student performance. Adapted from *Survey of Enacted Curriculum Training Material* by J. Smithson, 2004, Madison: Wisconsin Center for Gifted Education Research, University of Wisconsin. Copyright 2004 by Wisconsin Center for Gifted Education Research. Adapted with permission.

Once students have an understanding of their objective, their creativity can flow as they develop ways to pursue and present their learning.

When creating your own extension lessons, or modifying existing ones, it is important to balance the DOK levels to address the learning needs of all students in the class. If you have a number of gifted and talented students in the class, include more activities at DOK Levels 3 and 4. If your class has a significant number of students working at or below grade level, include several activities with DOK Levels 1 and 2, but also several Level 3 and 4 activities.

Pretesting to Determine Levels

Remember that teachers are not required to teach the standards to every student. Rather, teachers are required to ensure mastery of the standards. Students who can demonstrate mastery do not need to sit through instruction in that content. It is critical, however, that teachers document when students achieve mastery of the regular curriculum to provide evidence that the students are not missing instruction they need.

When teachers provide formative assessments they activate prior knowledge. This serves several purposes. First, it gives us the data needed to assign students to appropriate learning activities. Secondly, activating prior knowledge generates both divergent and convergent thinking, as students draw from background information to synthesize with new understandings—a critical aspect of activities involving strategic and extended thinking in DOK Levels 3 and 4.

Within Chapters 2–6 you will find examples of informal pretesting techniques teachers can use to determine the level of challenge students will need within a specific area. Teachers then use this formative assessment data to form flexible learning groups and to assign students to different activities according to DOK levels.

Presentation Methods and Projects

The activity formats, presentation methods, and projects that demonstrate learning will vary dramatically. In most activities, the presentation method and/or project is student directed, which allows for further differentiation of the content. Students use multiple resources, technologies, and presentation formats to demonstrate their understanding within the more complex activities. The activities guide the project design for the student; they are described in a way that allows students to decide the process, format, or method of presentation.

Sample Lesson: World Cultures

NCSS Standard
- o   I. Culture

CCSS ELA Standards
- o   RH.6-8.4
- o   RH.6-8.9
- o   WHST.6-8.7
- o   WHST.6-8.8
- o   WHST.6-8.9

Extension Activity

Research the religious, spiritual, or cultural beliefs of the selected culture and trace the origins of those beliefs into the history of this culture, going back to the ancient civilizations that were dominant in this part of the world (DOK 3).

Imagine assigning this type of learning activity. After considering the task, students will most likely start asking you for details on how to present the information. This is where you step back and facilitate the learning process, not guide it. Trust that the format will materialize during the research. Students should focus on the content, the task, and their background knowledge. With this focus, students can formulate the framework of how to present their understanding of the material. The following examples of projects created for this activity show how the presentation formats can vary.

Student Project 1

Micah decided to compare and contrast two cultures from different parts of the world. He researched themes found in their religious and cultural beliefs seeking to find a connection related to the origins of the cultures. He created a presentation demonstrating how the beliefs of two seemingly different cultures evolved over the course of time from similar belief structures.

Student Project 2

Yoko, whose parents are from Japan, chose to focus on the Japanese culture experienced in Japan and for those who immigrated to the United States. Specifically, she studied how the spiritual and cultural beliefs became interwoven over the past 70 years. She related these beliefs to the cultural climates during these different time periods. Yoko interviewed family members and family friends to obtain first person accounts. She then documented their experiences and perspectives within the time period. Yoko turned this DOK 3 activity into a DOK 4 by increasing the level of complexity.

As noted, the range of presentation methods students can use to report on or demonstrate their learning increases significantly with the level of challenge in the extension activities. With higher level activities, students need self-reflective skills that allow them to self-direct, monitor their progress, and evaluate their understanding. These critical thinking skills expand their opportunities and encourage the creative learning process.

Possible Project Formats

When working on activities, especially those in DOK Levels 2 through 4, students will need to determine how they want to demonstrate their learning. Project formats may take the form of digital or physical presentations. Digital presentations can be created in PowerPoint, Prezi, Keynote, website creations, or numerous other programs and applications. Physical presentations or demonstrations may involve reports, debates, speeches, editorials, essays, charts, oral presentations, or other displays.

Have students decide the presentation format for themselves whenever possible. This gives them practice evaluating options, planning, problem solving, and self-monitoring. Make suggestions when asked, but allow students to experience productive struggle in this process. This includes the opportunity to not succeed easily, an important step in the learning process. Later, when evaluating the project, you can discuss possible ways to improve the next time. The content, task, and the student's preferred learning styles will influence the project format.

You will find it helpful to keep both digital and physical samples of products/projects from various types of formats and from the different DOK levels. Make them accessible to students working on extension lessons to give them ideas for their own. Students working at all levels get excited about contributing to the sample bank!

Recognize that the extension projects will vary depending on what is being asked. The choice of format and content will also vary. Students will use multiple resources, technologies, and varied presentation formats to demonstrate their level of understanding in the more complex activities. Consider the following contrasting ways three students approached and demonstrated their learning within the same learning activity.

Sample Activity

Explain or demonstrate how all of the elements in a particular novel either worked together to enhance the quality of the novel or were in conflict to detract from the novel's quality (DOK 2).

Lonnie's Project

Lonnie created a video where he discussed each element in the context of the book *Fahrenheit 451*. He used video clips and animation to demonstrate how each element affected the novel. He then overlaid different elements to construct a visual of how the different elements enhanced the quality of the novel. Lonnie took what could have been a DOK Level 2 activity that focused on a skill or concept and made it a more complex Level 3 activity that required strategic thinking.

Yesenia's Project

Yesenia wrote an essay deconstructing her favorite scene from her novel *The Diary of Anne Frank*. She demonstrated how the elements created the scene's tone and feeling. She then deconstructed a less favored scene and compared how the interplay of the elements created a starkly contrasting tone. In the conclusion, she summarized how the contrasting elements worked to enhance and detract from the quality of the complete novel. Yesenia also made the project more complex.

David's Project

David's more traditional approach with the activity was sufficiently challenging for him. He made a chart identifying each of the elements. He created the headings and then wrote examples from the book *Holes* under each heading. David then listed three ways that the elements enhanced the quality of the novel and three ways it detracted from the novel. His teacher helped him formulate the plan.

Lonnie, Yesenia, and David all enjoyed the activity and all benefited from their ability to individualize their learning process. Best yet, they were all studying the same topic in a different way and with very little planning from the teacher. In fact, the teacher did not create the lesson herself. She accessed this extension activity from a digital repository that teachers throughout the district were adding to during the year.

Tech Integration

Today's learners are truly digital natives. Nearly all students in our classrooms today, K–12, were born in the 21st century. They glide through apps, texts, and tweets more easily than picking up a pencil. They learn using laptops, tablets, and their phones. Integrating technology into the learning environment must be an inherent aspect of instruction if students are to be prepared to succeed in tomorrow's world.

Providing students with relevant technology-integrated learning opportunities reflects today's curriculum and instruction. Adding a technology component for the sake of technology does not suffice. For authentic learning in the 21st century, teachers must train students in the strategies for conducting strong Internet searches, teach how to evaluate the validity of a source, provide guidance on Netiquette, hone the mechanics of sharing documents and developing presentations, as well as utilize the skill of computational thinking in the development of coding activities. These authentic learning experiences extend, expand, and allow students to exhibit their understandings. The student-directed nature of the activities necessitates access to technology for research and for the creation and presentation of the projects.

Project-Based Learning and Performance-Based Assessment

Project Based Learning (PBL) provides students with real-world learning scenarios that are both teacher and student designed. PBL engages students in the process of working on complex tasks over an extended period of time. Many of the activities contained here are similar in structure. They require that students investigate and then respond in detail by explaining a complex question or suggesting a solution to a real-world problem.

Project-based learning empowers students to embed 21st-century competencies and in-depth inquiry into significant content to deepen their understandings. Extension lessons can provide an avenue through which students engage in this type of student-directed learning. Many of the extension lessons can easily be extended further and developed into full PBL units, and some of the activities within the lessons reflect a simplified version of PBL. The extension lessons presented here are designed to provide:

> - significant learning challenges,
> - individualized pacing,
> - student responsibility,
> - task prioritization,
> - relevance, and
> - collaborative exchanges.

All of these goals are inherent in a comprehensive project-based unit.

Current and emerging innovative practices in the workplace require new ways to complete work and solve problems; they require the ability to address issues not yet known. To meet this challenge, student assessments need to move from forced choices of known options, like multiple-choice questions, to performance-based assessments, which deal in unknowns. Students must be able to apply their content knowledge using creative and critical thinking skills to analyze and find solutions to problems they have not previously encountered.

The project-based learning approach found in the extension lessons allows students to demonstrate their learning in relevant and authentic ways. Beyond standardized assessments of content knowledge, performance-based assessments allow teachers to measure students' habits of mind. This assessment format requires the use of higher order thinking skills to perform, create, or produce an artifact with real-world application.

Performance-based assessment moves the assessment process closer to a true demonstration of *how* students learn. This method challenges teachers to alter their instructional practices to emphasize student collaboration and increases the focus on written communication, problem solving, and real-world, hands-on activities. Both teachers and students increase self-reflection with this process.

Grading Extension Activities

"How do I grade these extension activities?" is a question teachers commonly ask when beginning to use them. Remember that many of these activities are designed to take students beyond the mastery of the grade-level standards. However, students should be assessed on their mastery of the grade-level content. If a student has earned full credit through his or her demonstration of grade-level standards, the extension activities should never lower the student's grade.

Extension lessons at the higher levels take students beyond the basic standards and engage them in productive struggle to enhance their understandings. The tasks should be rigorous and push students out of their comfort zones. Oftentimes their open-endedness allows for interpretation, in which case students develop a demonstration of learning that best addresses their areas of strength. This approach to learning can be difficult to assess; oftentimes, there is no "right" or "wrong" way to complete an activity. This is especially true with DOK Levels 3 and 4 activities.

Do not squelch creativity by imposing strict or punitive grading practices. Students should be given the opportunity to push themselves without fear that their efforts will negatively impact their grade. Extension activities can be assessed using a rubric that provides students with a clear understanding of the expectations of the assignment (see appendix, p. 239). Student effort and a measurement of progress are critical factors in their assessment.

Identification of clear indicators of performance are needed when designing a rubric to assess the varied aspects of an extension lesson. In most instances an analytic rubric will provide the depth of information needed in the assessment. In some cases, when an overall assessment is sought, a holistic rubric will provide the needed data.

The purpose of a rubric is not only to evaluate but also to help students enhance their level of performance by providing a guide to success. Rubrics can be used to assess students' thinking skills, depth of understanding, and ability to apply knowledge. A rubric provides the student, the parents, and the teacher with a clear look at documented expectations. Numerous online tools exist that support teachers in creating rubrics to use in the assessment process. The rubric can be as simple or as complex as desired by varying the depth of complexity of the activity, the objective, and the amount of work required for the activity, and other purposes related to the curriculum.

The key to a strong rubric lays in the clarity of the indicators. When designing a rubric, as with any assessment tool, begin with the standards to be assessed. Next, break the project into elements to be evaluated. Keep the number of elements manageable as including too many elements can be overwhelming for the student and the teacher.

Determining how mastery of the standard will be assessed in the rubric and the manner in which each element will be demonstrated follows a simple process. Identify the elements in terms of a desired project. For most educators, this represents a "3" on the rubric scale. If the students were to go beyond this expectation, consider what components they would enhance. These enhancements move the student from a demonstration that meets the standard(s) to one that exceeds, or to a "4" on the rubric scale. Completing the criteria for "2" and "1" are accomplished by identifying portions of the components that are lacking. For example, if the mastery requirement means the students produce a well-developed summary supported with a minimum of four examples, the student who writes a summary but provides two examples would not meet the mastery requirement and would earn a "2." The rubric provided in Figure 1.2 is an example used to assess critical thinking skills within a given unit.

Embedding a Self-Reflective Learning Process

The level of independence inherent in the extension lessons requires that students develop self-management skills and metacognitive abilities. Teachers can help students attain these skills by developing self-reflective processes. The varying levels of complexity within the extension lessons and the complexity within some of the problems can help build the self-regulation skills needed for self-reflection.

When working with extension lessons, students develop critical thinking, problem-solving, collaboration, self-direction, and creativity skills. Attention to these skills impacts the *process* of learning rather than the specific content being learned.

Critical Thinking

Apply critical thinking skills to solve problems, make informed decisions, and interpret events.

Rubric Element	4	3	2	1
Identifies and summarizes the problem/question	Problem/question identified accurately; well-developed summary	Problem/question identified accurately; brief summary	Problem/question identified accurately; poor summary or identifies incorrect problem/question	Does not identify or provide summary of problem/question
Identifies and assesses the quality of supporting data and evidence	Well-developed discussion of evidence for accuracy, relevance and completeness; clear fact/opinion distinction	Evidence examined and quality discussed; distinction made between fact and opinion	Repetition of provided information; limited distinction between fact and opinion	Does not identify or assess quality of evidence
Identifies and takes into account influence of the context	Accurately identifies and gives a well-developed explanation of contextual issues	Accurately identifies and gives an explanation of possible contextual issues	Contextual issues not explained; information in list format; inaccurate information	Does not identify or consider contextual issues
Demonstrates high-level thinking by interpreting the author's meaning or bias	Accurately identifies the author's meaning and/or potential bias; provides well-developed explanation	Accurately identifies conclusions, implications, and consequences; brief summary	Does not explain; inaccurate information; limited scope in summary	No information about author's meaning or possible bias
Identifies and evaluates conclusions, implications, and consequences	Accurately identifies conclusions, implications, and consequences with well-developed explanation; reflects on conclusions	Accurately identifies conclusions, implications, and consequences; brief summary	Does not explain; inaccurate information; limited scope in summary	Does not identify or evaluate any conclusions, implications, or consequences

Figure 1.2. Sample rubric. Adapted from *Washington State University Critical Thinking Rubric* by Washington State University Critical Thinking Project, 2001, Pullman, WA: The Center for Teaching, Learning, Technology, and General Education Programs, Washington State University. Copyright 2001 by Washington State University.

They are skills that, when well developed, enhance and elevate the level of understanding in whatever content area is being studied.

Accustom students to use and reflect on these skills to strengthen and support desired learning behaviors. When teachers develop a strong understanding of these skills, they naturally embed them into instruction. In so doing, teachers typically begin emphasizing specific terminology related to the skills. This process helps students derive a more thorough understanding of the content they are learning, particularly when engaged in extension activities in the higher DOK levels.

To focus student and teacher attention on the process of learning and how 21st-century skills embed into all curricular areas, address and emphasize the following skills:

> self-direction,
> problem solving,
> collaboration,
> critical thinking, and
> creativity.

These skills assist students in learning how to manage their time and attention, set and complete goals, and monitor the efficacy of their efforts. These skills become critical for students working on extension lessons whether they are working independently, with a partner, or in a small group. The lists shown here provide specific objectives for teachers to emphasize for this purpose.

Self-Direction

Malcolm Knowles (1975) defined self-directed learning:

In its broadest meaning, self-directed learning describes a process by which individuals take the initiative, with or without the assistance of others, in diagnosing their learning needs, formulating learning goals, identifying human and material resources for learning, choosing and implementing appropriate learning strategies, and evaluating learning outcomes. (p. 18)

Of primary importance in this definition of self-directed learning is that the learner takes the initiative to pursue a specific learning experience and the responsibility for completing their learning. These skills can be explicitly taught and will help students develop the practices they need when working on extension lessons.

Teachers can emphasize the following objectives when teaching students to develop their abilities for self-direction:

> set challenging, achievable goals and identify and access the resources necessary to achieve the goals;

➤ manage time and resources in an efficient manner to achieve goals;

➤ review progress and learning experiences to resolve problems that may be interfering with achieving goals;

➤ ask others for feedback and seriously consider their ideas when revising work;

➤ be determined to find an answer or solution to a problem and monitor commitment to the goals;

➤ identify and describe the criteria and performance standards for quality work;

➤ identify strengths and weaknesses of one's work in clear terms and identify areas for improvement; and

➤ reflect to set new goals and effectively incorporate information learned from successes and struggles.

These objectives allow students to create and keep to a schedule, monitor progress, and produce quality work. They also help students build independence and strengthen the ability to persevere when working on challenging tasks.

Problem Solving

A major goal in education is to enable students to use what they have learned to solve problems in new situations. Problem solving has been described as "cognitive processing directed at achieving a goal when no solution or method is obvious to the problem solver" (Mayer & Wittrock, 2006). Problem solving is a process that involves reasoning, decision-making, and thinking critically. Many of the extension activities in this book require that students use these problem-solving strategies.

Teachers can emphasize the following objectives when teaching students to build their abilities to problem solve:

➤ carefully analyze all of the characteristics of a problem before beginning to solve it;

➤ identify important information needed to solve complex problems;

➤ anticipate different kinds of problems in complicated projects and determine ways to address the problems before they occur;

➤ use the strategies learned, along with subject-area knowledge, to solve problems; and

➤ reflect on problem-solving processes, evaluate the learning process, and make changes when necessary.

The ability to problem solve is critical for students working independently on learning activities that are abstract and open-ended. Due to their open-ended nature, some extension lesson activities in higher DOK levels necessitate that students monitor progress, focus on their process, and make adjustments when needed. Redirecting their efforts helps students refine the quality of their work, further develop their ideas, and scrutinize the purpose of the activity.

Collaboration

When students work collaboratively to solve problems they share knowledge and develop skills that can lead to deeper learning and understanding. Collaborative learning has been shown to result in higher student achievement, higher self-esteem, and higher motivation for all students across all socioeconomic and cultural backgrounds. Monique Devane (Edutopia, 2012) explained, "Individual work can be a great way to master content, but group work empowers and enables a student's cultivation of resilience."

When working collaboratively, students see each other as resources where they can test their own theories, determine if they are on the right track, and develop habits of mind. Keep in mind that students need guidance to learn to work together effectively. Teachers can emphasize the following objectives when teaching students to develop their abilities of collaboration:

- actively contribute to the group by participating in discussions, accept and perform required tasks, help the group set goals, and direct the group in meeting goals;
- share ideas and contribute information appropriate to the topic and encourage other members to share their ideas;
- balance listening and speaking;
- take into account other people's feelings and ideas; and
- participate in the group discussion assessing how well they are working together.

Extension activities at all DOK levels can involve students working with partners or in small groups. However, some students, particularly those with high ability, face challenges when working with peers. These students may need to develop strategies for working collaboratively with others. They may also need to learn how to listen, how to take turns talking, and how to monitor oneself and others when working with peers.

Critical Thinking

Thinking is not driven by answers but by questions. The extension activities provide questions that require students to think critically as opposed to simply answering a question. Richard Paul (2007), director of Research and Professional Development at the Center for Critical Thinking, defined critical thinking as, "thinking that analyzes thought, that assesses thought, and that transforms thought for the better . . . It's thinking about thinking while thinking in order to think better."

This process improves the ability to solve problems. Teachers can emphasize the following objectives when teaching students to build critical thinking abilities:

➤ identify the most important parts of the information being studied;
➤ use multiple strategies for evaluating the reliability of different kinds of sources;
➤ use subject area knowledge and personal experiences to make connections and draw inferences between content areas; and
➤ clearly explain an opinion on a topic in speaking and in writing and give good reasons for it.

Given the independent nature of the activities, students working at the higher DOK levels need the ability to think critically, which involves analyzing information and supporting their methodology. They will often need to rely on past learning experiences and consider prior knowledge when completing the learning activities. To accomplish this requires that students discern and evaluate relevancy of information when synthesizing material. Teacher attention toward developing this ability helps students self-direct and problem solve when analyzing information at deeper levels.

Creativity

To foster and nurture the growth of creativity, Dr. E. Paul Torrance (1990) advised teachers to "encourage curiosity, exploration, experimentation, fantasy, questioning, testing, and the development of creative talents" (p. 4). These processes should be inherent in all aspects of learning and in all subject areas. Teachers can emphasize the following objectives when helping students develop creativity:

➤ use knowledge and skills in the subject matter to generate possible ideas;
➤ seek out new experiences without worrying about what others think or whether mistakes will be made;
➤ have confidence in one's own ability to determine if ideas are worth pursuing;
➤ add the necessary concrete details to an idea to make it a successful product or performance; and
➤ use language in meaningful and novel ways to move, inspire, entertain, inform, and persuade others.

Creativity abounds in high-ability students. However, the propensity to expand on creativity has the potential to deter students from their learning goals. Extension lessons are only valid when they further the understanding of the content being considered. When students stray too far from the learning objectives, the lesson can become more of an unrelated enrichment activity rather than an extension of the objective.

Instill the goals of creativity and mastering learning objectives in all students. Students working on activities at the higher DOK levels especially need to develop these skills. Encouraging a self-reflective process with students helps prepare students for lifelong learning.

Teacher Planning Meetings

Holding regularly scheduled planning meetings for teachers builds a system within the school that offers them ongoing support. These meetings can provide teachers opportunities to share teaching strategies and lesson plans with each other and brainstorm solutions to challenges they face. In current professional development language, this structure is typically in the form of a Professional Learning Community (PLC). Peer coaching can be a logical part of this model and an integral part of school-based PLCs.

We recommend holding planning meetings at least once a month, but meeting more often may be desired. Having a scheduled time to plan together helps prepare all teachers when adopting new instructional methods, such as those demonstrated here. Teachers feel more confident knowing there are others at their school with whom they can consult when they need assistance or validation. Even experienced teachers appreciate this collaborative time to gain new ideas and create and share extension lessons with each other.

Building a Shared Lesson Repository

Creating extension lessons can take time, but once they have been created, a teacher can use them forever. If there are other teachers in your school or district using this instructional format, consider creating a shared digital repository where you can archive and access each other's plans and projects on your school's or district's server or Intranet. When building a repository of extension lessons, create a folder for each content area: language arts, math, history, and science. You may want to create two folders within each content area: one for plans and one for sample projects.

Creating a shared extension lesson repository can provide all district teachers with access to innovative instructional methods, advanced and differentiated curriculum, and systems for communication, collaborative learning, and using achievement data.

A shared repository exposes teachers to instructional strategies that engage, challenge, and enrich all students. This instructional support method can increase student collaboration, communication, critical thinking, and creativity throughout the school or district. It can also motivate all teachers to incorporate higher level instructional objectives and strategies into everyday teaching for all students.

Table 1.1
Common Terminology

Term	Definition
Depth of Knowledge (DOK)	DOK is a reference to the complexity of mental processing that must occur to answer a question, perform a task, or generate a product.
Bloom's taxonomy (Bloom's)	A classification system used to define and distinguish different levels of human cognition (i.e., thinking, learning, and understanding).
English language arts (ELA)	Refers to the Reading and Language Arts components of the Common Core State Standards.
Common Core State Standards (CCSS)	A set of high-quality academic expectations that define the knowledge and skills all students should master by the end of each grade level in order to be on track for success in college and career.
Performance-based assessments (PBA)	A form of assessment that evaluates the acquisition and application of knowledge, skills, and work habits through the performance of tasks that are meaningful and engaging to students.
Response to Intervention (RtI)	A multitier approach to the early identification and support of students with learning and behavior needs. The RtI process begins with high-quality instruction and universal screening of all children in the general education classroom.
Common formative assessments (CFA)	An assessment or set of assessment items created collaboratively by a team of teachers responsible for the same grade level or course.
Mathematical Practices (MP)	Mathematical Practices describe the way in which mathematical understandings are acquired. These practices rest on important "processes and proficiencies" with longstanding importance in mathematics education.

Terminology Today

With changing times come changing terminology. Several of the terms used in this chapter reflect the verbiage of today's evolving educational environment. Table 1.1 includes a few commonly used terms that pertain to the learning activities that follow in Chapters 2–6.

English Language Arts Extension Lessons

Introduction

The extension lessons in this chapter allow middle school English teachers to further explore the elements of the CCSS for ELA (NGA & CCSSO, 2010a). The teacher's role is to instruct students in the nuances of language and provide a structure that allows students to develop their critical and creative thinking processes.

Preassessment

You will find that preassessing skills in English instruction will occur less frequently than in other content areas, such as mathematics and history, as other content areas involve more explicit content. Preassessing in English is more informal. For example, you may ask students to produce a quick write showing their understandings of a particular element or administer a short quiz to determine student understandings of key terms. These preassessments provide a structure through which flexible learning groups can be created. The preassessment data can also be used to guide the selection of extension lesson activities.

Sample Lesson

In the sample lesson below, students engage with the poem "Nothing Gold Can Stay" by Robert Frost and explore the use of figurative language and symbolism. This leads them to a video clip from the movie *Up,* "Love Story," selected based on its lack of dialogue. The story is told completely through visual images. The symbolism is dynamic, allowing students to gain a visual perspective. The two pieces are then tied together and students are asked to determine how each author used literary techniques to move the audience to understanding.

In this example, the teacher has chosen to engage learners with the extension lessons after the lesson. Student performance on class activities and in the Socratic Seminar provides the data used to determine appropriate DOK levels. An extension lesson is then used to expand students' understandings by providing options of increased complexity.

Consider the extension lesson, "Irony, Ambiguity, and Symbolism." The extension's DOK Level 1 (recall) activity asks students to identify the symbolism associated with several holidays of their choice and explain how the symbolism is portrayed in their lives. This activity provides a basic level of complexity while connecting students to the topic being addressed. The DOK Level 3 activity requires that students identify figurative language within a recently read novel and evaluate the author's purpose in using the particular figurative language style. Additionally, the students demonstrate how the language used advances the theme of the novel. This level of complexity requires a much higher cognitive ability and deeper reasoning skills. By coupling the lessons directly taught within the classroom with extension lesson activities, students are afforded a wider range of experiences through which to deepen their understandings.

ELA Sample Lesson

Objective
> Develop an understanding of the impact of imagery in multiple formats.

CCSS ELA Standards
- o   R.1–7
- o   R.9–10
- o   SL.1
- o   W. 1, 3–5, 8–9

Key Vocabulary
- Visual imagery

Materials
- Poem: "Nothing Gold Can Stay" by Robert Frost
- Video Clip: *Up*, "Love Story"

Text Component
- Teacher reads the poem aloud.
- Second reading: Students read with partners.
- Teacher asks: Is this poem literal?
- Students reread the poem, looking for specific details that demonstrate the symbolism in the poem.
- Pair and share: In predetermined pairs students share their evidence.
- Whole class: Students identify four symbols used in the poem.
- Quick write: Students respond to the following: What point is Frost making? How does he use imagery and symbolism to build meaning? Do you agree with his premise?
- Socratic seminar based on the quick write topic. Students make notes of their evidence prior to the seminar.

Video Component
- Students view the "Love Story" clip from the movie *Up*, available at https://www.youtube.com/watch?v=UTBQYAE-pMK.
- Second viewing: Students:
  - identify four examples of symbolism;
  - identify four examples of imagery; and
  - with a partner, share their thoughts.

- Identify the role that symbolism plays in the clip. With a partner or table group, identify the symbolism and what is being represented. Student teams will share out loud and discuss.
- Journal: Why do you feel that the screenwriter chose to create this piece without dialogue?

Extension Lesson
As students develop their journal entry, the teacher will work with students individually to guide them to the DOK level of extension appropriate to meet their challenge needs. Students will then be provided time to work on their extension lesson selection.

LESSON 2.1
American Studies

CCSS ELA Standards

- » RH.6-8.2
- » RH.6-8.6
- » RI.7.7
- » RI.7.8

Activities

- » Create a set of questions and answers from the current unit of study for the class to use in its next academic bowl game or other quiz game (DOK 1).
- » Illustrate and describe several articles of clothing that would have been worn by five characters in a novel about this time period (DOK 1).
- » Create a newsletter that contains stories and features articles about actual events written in ways authentic to the period of time you are studying (DOK 2).
- » Compare and contrast how schools were run during this time period with how they are run today (DOK 2).
- » Study *The Timetables of History* by Bernard Grun (2005). Design a way to make your classmates aware of what was occurring in the rest of the world during a significant period of American history (DOK 3).
- » Evaluate the historical accuracy of a novel read. Compare evidence in the text to historical facts from the same place and time period to support your conclusions (DOK 3).
- » Investigate and report on ways in which the expansion of multiculturalism in America has impacted our politics and literature (DOK 4).
- » Write a historically based short story from the time period you are studying. Accurately portray the characters, location, setting, theme, conflict, dialogue, point of view, etc., within the time period in which it is set. Emphasize and include in your text discussion an area or topic of interest you have related to this time period. Include the critical elements contained in short stories in your work (DOK 4).

LESSON 2.2
Author Studies

CCSS ELA Standards

- » RL.7.6
- » RL.8.5
- » RI.8.6

Activities

- » Research and describe the skills needed to be a successful and effective editor (DOK 1).
- » Investigate the different routes several authors have taken during their careers (DOK 1).
- » Locate interviews of the author of the work you recently completed reading. Identify conflicting information and consider reasons for the conflict. In your presentation, discuss how you gained insight into the author's style (DOK 2).
- » Identify other pieces the author has written that do not follow the style he or she used in this piece. Note the similarities and differences between styles in a format of your choosing (DOK 2).
- » Contact the author of your recently read book. Before doing so, create a list of questions to ask that might illuminate this person's style, messages, method of writing, or other aspects in which you are interested. How does the information you learned alter your initial impression of his or her work? Report on your findings (DOK 2).
- » Examine the publishing business, including decisions to publish, royalty arrangements, inventory issues, and how the Internet is impacting traditional publishing. In your project, include your opinion on the future of publishing (paper) books as opposed to digital books (DOK 3).
- » Select three novels written by the same author. Identify the theme developed in each novel. Compare how the theme was developed in each novel. What patterns do you see? How did the author's writing style influence theme development? Prepare a paper or presentation with your findings (DOK 4).
- » "Meet the Author" websites can be marketing tools. Research several sites and describe how they are used to promote the author. Create a website for an author designed to promote specific current and future work (DOK 4).

LESSON 2.3
Cause and Effect

CCSS ELA Standards

- » W.6.2.a
- » W.7.2.a
- » RI.7.5

Activities

- » Select a nonfiction text. Identify and record 5–10 cause and effect relationships (DOK 1).
- » Read a picture book that illustrates cause and effect. Select key sentences and diagram the cause and the effect in each sentence. Discuss the author's purpose (DOK 2).
- » In a book you are currently reading or have just finished reading, describe how a specific cause and effect relationship was critical to the turning point in the novel (DOK 2).
- » Relate a cause and effect relationship in a story you just read to a similar event in your life. In your presentation, draw similarities and discuss different outcomes that could have occurred in either event (DOK 3).
- » Listen to the cause and effect song titled "Cowboy Logic," available at http://www.songsforteaching.com/math/logicreasoning/if-then-cause-effect.php. Create a third verse of the song communicating three new examples of cause and effect relationships (DOK 3).
- » Create a cause and effect concentration game related to a book read by your class. Record each cause on a note card and its effect on a note card of a different color. Create at least 20 pairs. Provide a clear set of directions and an answer key for your game (DOK 3).
- » Select a Norman Rockwell painting. Write a hypothetical narrative about the story illustrated through the painting. Record a cause and effect relationship within your paragraph that fits with the time period (DOK 4).
- » Implicit versus explicit: Visit http://www.byrdseed.com/wp-content/uploads/Portrait_of_Dr._Gachet.jpg. Select two of the paintings. Create an implicit statement about what you see, such as describing the person's mood. Then create some explicit statements, such as how you know the person feels (peaceful, sad, upset, lonely, etc.). Prove it (DOK 4).

LESSON 2.4
Theme

CCSS ELA Standards

» RL.8.2
» RL.8.5

Activities

» Locate and describe several passages in the literary piece that strongly convey the theme (DOK 1).
» Investigate and explain the origins of the use of the word "theme" (DOK 1).
» Select a story you really enjoyed reading. Describe the theme. Predict how the story would change if a different theme were used (DOK 2).
» Identify and describe any theme, such as love, ethics, death, betrayal, friendship, etc. as it is portrayed in visual or graphic modes throughout the selected text. How does the theme evolve (DOK 2)?
» Locate and describe several passages in a literary piece that strongly convey the theme. How is the theme portrayed (DOK 3)?
» Evaluate how various cultures use themes in mythology to represent the values and mores of their society (DOK 3).
» Identify and explain examples of how simile, metaphor, and other types of figurative language reinforce the theme of a particular piece of literature. Provide several specific examples. Assess the extent to which these literary devices reinforce the theme (DOK 3).
» Study themes in musical selections or categories of music. Describe specific moments/segments in the piece of music that state or reinforce the theme on which the composer was building (DOK 4).

LESSON 2.5
Vocabulary in Text

CCSS ELA Standards

» RL.6-8.4
» L.7.4

Activities

» Using vocabulary words from a current unit of study, create three vocabulary webs that include several of the following elements: the word's definition, root words, affixes, part of speech, synonyms, antonyms, an example, a sentence. Use each of the elements at least two times (DOK 1).

» Identify at least 10 words germane to the content of the text you are studying. Represent each of your words in such a way that they demonstrate the meaning of the word. For example, "submerged" might be drawn partially under water (DOK 1).

» Revise a current piece of work to incorporate figurative language (DOK 2).

» Reflect on a book you just read. Compose a simile related to the book and create an illustration that depicts its meaning (DOK 2).

» Invent a new word. Include its definition, root word, affix, part of speech, synonyms, antonyms, an example, a sentence using the word, and the context in which you believe the word would be appreciated (DOK 2).

» Compare and contrast figurative and literal language from your current reading. Consider when authors might rely more heavily on each of these and discuss how the meaning and message differs for each (DOK 3).

» Write a letter to the editor regarding a current issue. The challenge will be that you may not use prefixes or suffixes. After completing your letter, rewrite it using prefixes and suffixes. Assess and discuss the difference between the two editorials (DOK 3).

» Study songs and poems that include various types of figurative language. Create a song or poem that includes figurative language, focusing on personification, similes, and idioms. Analyze the difference between songs and poems that contain figurative language and those that do not (DOK 4).

LESSON 2.6
Persuasive Writing

CCSS ELA Standards

- » W.8.1.a
- » W.8.2.b
- » RI.8.8
- » RI.8.5

Activities

- » Describe elements that make persuasive writing effective. Identify and list these elements in a famous speech (DOK 1).
- » Select a famous debate and study the assumed winner. Identify elements you feel led to the winner's success (DOK 2).
- » Construct a compelling advertisement that contains a logical fallacy (DOK 2).
- » Study possible solutions to a problem that interests you and create an argument for the one(s) most likely to succeed (DOK 3).
- » Evaluate the jury's decision in a court case that interests you and create a persuasive document to prove the decision was correct or incorrect (DOK 3).
- » Select a current editorial that intrigues you. Construct an argument based on the position presented in the editorial. Then create a political cartoon based on an argument from the editorial page (DOK 3).
- » Study the reasoning, word choice, and point of view of two countries' declarations of independence. Identify obstacles that may have surfaced in the years following their original publication (DOK 4).
- » You have the opportunity to hold the world's attention for 30 minutes. Compose the speech you would deliver to persuade the world to follow/adopt your stated position on an issue of your choice. Identify several obstacles (such as people's perceptions or stances) you are attempting to influence (DOK 4).

LESSON 2.7
Poetry Elements

CCSS ELA Standards

- » RL.7.4
- » RL.7.5
- » RL.8.4

Activities

For the following activities students will either be assigned poems to study or will be able to select a poem to use.

- » Identify several interesting words used in the poem. Research and report on their origins (DOK 1).
- » Determine the classification regarding structure to which this poem belongs. Describe how the structure provides meaning to the poem (DOK 2).
- » Rearrange parts of a poem to determine how the meaning is affected by the sequence of ideas. Describe your findings (DOK 2).
- » Select a poem to study. Then find another poem of the same type that relates to a similar theme or purpose of the poem you first studied. Identify and explain the similarities and differences (DOK 3).
- » Compare and contrast the rhythm and rhyme scheme of the poem with that of a piece of music written on the same or a related theme. Draw inferences as to how they both depict the topic in their own ways (DOK 3).
- » Find a piece of art that is concerned with the same or related topic as a poem you select for study. Analyze how effectively the topic is handled in both forms. Include specific references from both pieces (DOK 3).
- » Select a poem of interest to you. Research the author and then examine several other poems from this author during the same time period. Consider and describe events from the poem in the context of the times. Determine the extent to which events in the poet's life are reflected in the poem (DOK 4).
- » Research and explain the historical context of a poem and analyze how your selected poem reflects that context. Compare this to the same historical context of a piece of music from the time. Discuss the themes and similarities and/or differences and how they reflect the time periods and sentiments in which they were written (DOK 4).

LESSON 2.8
Poetic Connections

CCSS ELA Standards

- » RL.7.4
- » RL.7.5
- » RL.8.4

Activities

- » Select and define four or five forms or structures in poetry. Identify a poem using each of these forms or structures. Describe what element(s) of each poem reflect that category (DOK 1).
- » Examine the connection between poetry and song lyrics in general. Contrast and compare the relationship between the two (DOK 2).
- » Select a poem in a genre of your choice. Use context clues in the poem to identify the author's purpose. Present examples of how the author accomplished this purpose. Cite evidence from the poem and also an inferred or symbolic allusion supporting the author's purpose (DOK 2).
- » Explore the connection between some poetry you admire and the author's personal life experiences. Defend the statement: "A poet must know something well in order to write well about it." This may be presented in a position paper or as an oral defense (DOK 3).
- » Take a poem written in language that is difficult to understand, such as Old English, and translate it into more contemporary language. Then compare the differences. How does changing the language change the meaning or tone of the poem (DOK 3)?
- » Investigate the likelihood of being able to make a living as a poet. Estimate the percentage of people who write poetry who actually can call poetry writing their profession. Analyze and describe reasons why people choose to write poetry even if it can't be profitable financially (DOK 3).
- » Compose an original poem. Include an analysis using the appropriate terminology and academic language (DOK 4).
- » Select a well-known poem of your preference. Research the time period and the social and/or political context in which it was written. Analyze how the poem reflects events and feelings of that time period (DOK 4).

LESSON 2.9
Writing Short Stories

CCSS ELA Standards

- » RL.7.3
- » RL.8.3
- » RL.7.4

Activities

- » Identify and define at least 10 vocabulary words from the story that were unfamiliar to you or that intrigued you while reading the story. Discuss how some of these words relate to the story (DOK 1).
- » Study another short story on a similar topic by another author. Using literary terms, report on the similarities and differences between authors and stories (DOK 2).
- » Suggest a different ending to the story that reflects another logical way the story might have ended if the same events took place. Describe how this change would alter the story (DOK 2).
- » Alter one of the story elements. Discuss why you selected to change this element. Consider and discuss the impact this change might have had on the characters or storyline (DOK 2).
- » Examine the author's background and relate pertinent information that you believe impacts the theme of the story (DOK 3).
- » Evaluate how the different backgrounds and cultures of the characters in the story impacted the events and outcome of the story (DOK 3).
- » Consider how this story could develop as a novel rather than a short story. Identify which parts would be most suited to developing. Defend your reasoning by describing how this development would serve a purpose (DOK 4).
- » Analyze how events from the time period of the work impacted the events in the story. Given the times, offer alternative possible pathways the events could have led to that would have dramatically changed the outcome of the story (DOK 4).

LESSON 2.10
Short Story Elements

CCSS ELA Standards

- » RL.7.3
- » RL.8.3
- » RL.7.4

Activities

- » Describe and explain the conflict or conflict(s) that drove the plot and the characters to evolve as they did (DOK 1).
- » Create a timeline illustrating the events in the plot. Make annotations showing how the events impacted other events (DOK 1).
- » Choose at least five terms from the list below. Cite an example from the story for each term and describe its impact on the story (DOK 2).

  - ◆ Suspense
  - ◆ Personification
  - ◆ Point of View
  - ◆ Foreshadowing
  - ◆ Simile
  - ◆ Voice
  - ◆ Coincidence

  - ◆ Metaphor
  - ◆ Tone
  - ◆ Inevitability
  - ◆ Hyperbole
  - ◆ Pun
  - ◆ Sensationalism
  - ◆ Allusion

- » Discuss the climax and falling action (denouement) in the story. Provide examples and describe how elements of each action add to the story (DOK 3).
- » Analyze and describe how the setting influences the conflict of the story and contributes to the development of the protagonist (DOK 3).
- » Convince an audience as to how the story's dialogue, events, and interactions reveal aspects of the protagonist or antagonist's character (DOK 3).
- » Create an alternative resolution to the conflict and an ending that resonates with the tone the author used. Discuss the reasoning behind your approach (DOK 4).
- » Analyze how the relationship between the antagonist and protagonist in two stories you've read is impacted by their experiences with one another and how it influences their decisions (DOK 4).

LESSON 2.11
Response to Literature

CCSS ELA Standards

» RL.6.3
» RL.8.2
» RL.8.3

Activities

» Describe how a main character changes over time. Cite evidence from the text to support your findings (DOK 1).

» Determine the cause and effect of a narrative hook in a given story. Describe how the causal events in the rising action are related to the cause and effect (DOK 2).

» Study biographical information about the author and determine what bias, if any, this author may have brought to the story he or she wrote. Give reasons for your conclusions (DOK 3).

» Research and explain how the rules of the "Freytag Pyramid" are illustrated in a novel of your choice. The "Freytag Pyramid" was developed by Gustav Freytag in 1861 to use with dramatic literature (DOK 3).

» Consider all the elements represented in the type of literature you are reading. Choose three that you believe the author handled exceptionally well. Explain why you selected these and provide rationale for your choices. Cite evidence from the text to support your claims (DOK 3).

» Study the author's style of using foreshadowing in the story. Note examples of any ambiguity from expected outcomes compared to actual outcomes (DOK 3).

» Select a piece of literature that resonates with you. It should be one that made you care deeply for the characters and develop a sincere interest in what would happen to them. Analyze the methods the author used to generate these responses and consider the author's purpose. Identify current events in the world that may elicit similar feelings. Discuss the connections (DOK 4).

» Identify another author from the same period who wrote the piece of literature you are studying. Consider the story from this other author's point of view. What elements might stay the same, which might change, and how would they change (DOK 4)?

LESSON 2.12
Shakespeare's Characters

CCSS ELA Standards

- » RL.8.3
- » RL.8.4
- » RL.8.7

Activities

For the activities in this extension lesson students will select a recently read Shakespearean play.

- » Identify character traits that represent stereotypes of people in Shakespeare's plays. List the traits. Then select specific Shakespearean character(s) and provide a description of the character(s). Include the name of the play(s) for the character(s) you describe (DOK 2).
- » Select several characters from Shakespearean plays. Research and identify the connections between them and archetypes in literature and history (DOK 2).
- » Explore the theme of honor. Create a dialogue discussing it between characters in a Shakespearean play. Use language true to the author, time, and genre (DOK 3).
- » Notice how the characters in the play use both 'high' and "low" language representative of different social classes of the time. Consider the benefits to the characters that can move between the two types of language. Identify examples of how several characters do this in one of more of Shakespeare's plays. In your discussion, note the characters, the play, and sample lines (DOK 3).
- » Select several metaphors and other uses of language that enhance the play. Use context clues to describe how their presence enhances the writing (DOK 3).
- » Shakespeare was believed to have followed the work of Raphael Holinshed in his book, *The Chronicles of England, Scotland, and Ireland* (2nd ed.), in 1587. Use other books that describe the same time period to find examples that verify the occurrence of selected events in Shakespeare's historical plays (DOK 3).
- » Locate and describe idioms Shakespeare uses that are still common in modern English usage, either in English speaking countries in Europe, or in the United States. Discuss how the meaning evolved during these timeframes.

Include your assumption as to why these phrases have endured over time (DOK 4).

» There have been whispers for many years that Shakespeare did not write all of his own plays. Research this assertion and create a position paper on the topic. Refer to evidence from the plays, and also from historical accounts, to support your position (DOK 4).

LESSON 2.13
Biography

CCSS ELA Standards

- » RI.6.9
- » RI.7.9
- » RI.7.8

Activities

- » Read two biographies of authors who have written in a specific category. Illustrate elements they have in common (DOK 1).
- » Prepare a biography of a person who was connected to a particular historical event your classmates are studying (DOK 2).
- » Create an annotated bibliography of biographies in a specific category, such as women, astronauts, child prodigies, musicians, inventors, sports heroes, and entertainers. Your purpose is to find a way to get others interested in reading the books (DOK 2).
- » Select a recently read biography to study. Identify several issues about which the subject would have been proud. From this, create his or her obituary and epitaph (DOK 2).
- » Illustrate the relationship between the subject's life and the time period in which he or she lived. Include information about specific events and how those events influenced the person's life (DOK 3).
- » Create an illustrated timeline showing major and minor events in the subject's life. Using cues from the biography, create a second layer of the timeline showing things the person might have wanted to do or accomplish. Consider obstacles or events that prevented the subject from achieving those desired accomplishments. Describe your findings in a brief summary discussion in the format of your choosing. Be sure that your audience will be able to distinguish between the two versions—real and hypothesized (DOK 3).
- » Using digital media, illustrate the "snapshot method" of biography, in which you show common themes or elements found in several biographies recently published (DOK 3).
- » Describe gender or ethnic issues in biographies written for your age group during the past few decades. Discuss the presence of these issues today and how they are reflected in life today (DOK 4).

LESSON 2.14
Novel Studies

CCSS ELA Standards

» RL.7.2
» RL.6.3
» RL.7.3

Activities

» Create a character map of the main characters using textual evidence to support your descriptions (DOK 1).

» Prepare and present information describing the customs and traditions of the characters and the time period of the novel you are reading (DOK 1).

» Select a recently read novel. Develop two fictitious interview or oral histories, one with a character that you admire and one for whom you had negative feelings. Explain why you feel the way you do about each character after completing the interview or oral history (DOK 2).

» Examine the physical surroundings of your novel's setting. Consider how the setting might have appeared in a different time period. Then predict how the story in the novel might have been different if the events had happened in another time period (DOK 2).

» Analyze several quotes from characters in your current novel as to their impact on other characters and events. Look for examples of how specific dialogue improved the storyline. Present your findings (DOK 3).

» Create an advertisement promoting a series of novels. Design it so that it will appeal to a wide variety of readers. Then discuss in writing how the series' themes reach those audiences and how you made that connection in your advertisement (DOK 4).

» Critique how the moral beliefs of the characters impacted their behavior and the events in the story. Include a discussion on how these beliefs influenced the story as a whole with attention toward the time period of the novel (DOK 4).

» Assume the novel you are studying will be made into a full-length feature movie at some time. Predict which events should be retained and which should be eliminated and then defend your predictions. Create one or two new events that might be included in a movie version and present them in a way that involves characters from the novel. Provide rationale for including these scenes by making connections to current events or issues (DOK 4).

LESSON 2.15
Novel Study Exploratory Activities

CCSS ELA Standards

» RL.6.3
» RL.7.2
» RL.7.3

Activities

» Create a wanted poster about the antagonist of the novel. Include his or her statistics, characteristics, and the motivation behind his or her actions (DOK 1).
» Create an ABC book where you cite one word for each letter of the element. Each of the words you cite must reflect an element of the novel (characters, setting, theme, etc.; DOK 1).
» Choose five "artifacts" from the book that best illustrate the tone, mood, theme, or main idea of the story. Create a digital "book bag" that includes these artifacts or symbols from the book. Explain their significance to the story (DOK 2).
» Choose a scene from the book that demonstrates a turning point for the protagonist. Create a script or a dramatic reading of the scene (DOK 2).
» Summarize the book by writing a comic book or storybook aimed at younger students or your classmates. Design a book cover depicting an event of the story for your comic or storybook (DOK 3).
» Create a board game focusing on the elements of the novel. Include the game rules and important events that happen throughout the plot. Use problems from the book as ways to move ahead or to be penalized. Present and then play (DOK 3).
» Write an alternative climax to the novel. Analyze how the falling action and resolution would change if the climax were different and include your justifications in your ending (DOK 3).
» Make a video or create a live performance of a program that reviews books and interviews authors. Work with a partner. One of you is the host of the program and the other is the author of the book. The host will give a synop-

sis of the book and ask questions to the author, such as what he or she was thinking and feeling when writing the book, his or her favorite part of the book, etc. The author will explain choices of setting, character, and motivation for writing the book. The audience may also ask questions for the author to answer (DOK 4).

LESSON 2.16
Survival Novels

CCSS ELA Standards

- » RL.6.10
- » RL.8.2
- » RL.8.3

Activities

- » Write to the author of your favorite survival novel to learn about the author's personal experiences within this genre. Write in care of his or her publisher (DOK 1).
- » Consider a survival technique used in the book you are reading. Research this survival technique used in a similar setting in real life. Assess the degree of accuracy to which the technique was displayed in the book (DOK 2).
- » Locate and view videos of Holocaust survivors' interviews. Identify and compare the characteristics they share with characters you have read about in survival novels (DOK 3).
- » Research real-life survival stories. Compare and contrast the character traits shared by these people with the characters in the survival novel you have been reading. How realistic was the character in the book compared to the person in the real survival story (DOK 3)?
- » After reading a survival book, identify the story's elements: plot, setting, characters, theme, author's purpose. Speculate on how some of these elements differ in this genre than they might in a different genre, such as mystery or historical fiction (DOK 3).
- » Well-known people sometimes need survival techniques to deal with constant recognition. Investigate and describe in detail ways in which they deal with this situation (DOK 3).
- » Investigate what it takes to survive and move on after a person experiences unwelcome attention that makes him or her easily recognizable for a long time. How might an author portray this type of survival in a story (DOK 4)?
- » Read a novel wherein people need to migrate from their homes to survive threatening situations. Relate this story to current news accounts of families fleeing their home countries seeking safety, political freedom, or a better life. Apply concepts from the novel to the real-life situations occurring today and investigate what is being done to assist those currently in need. Analyze how current-day efforts might have assisted those in the novel you read (DOK 4).

LESSON 2.17
Chasing Vermeer

CCSS ELA Standards

- » RL.6.5
- » RL.7.1
- » RL.7.2

Activities

- » Twelve is an important number, especially toward the end of the novel. Make a list of everything that comes in sets of 12, or by the dozen in the novel and then add other examples from life outside the novel (DOK 1).
- » A big part of the story revolves around ads placed in the newspaper. Imagine yourself as either Petra or Calder right after the mystery is solved. Write a newspaper account of their adventure (DOK 1).
- » Create an ABC profile about the novel. Use a word associated with every letter of the alphabet. Display creatively (DOK 1).
- » Illustrator Brett Helquist talks about the challenge of hiding the pentominoes in his illustrations. Create a new drawing, either on paper or digitally, to conceal a pentomino or other secret image or message in the picture. Describe your process in creating the concealment (DOK 2).
- » Look at the illustrations with fresh eyes. Select one illustration from the novel and write a caption for it that has nothing to do with the story of *Chasing Vermeer* (DOK 2).
- » If you were in charge of turning this book into a movie, which scenes would be most important to include in the movie adaptation that maintain the theme and main idea of the text as well as the development of the characters? Justify your responses (DOK 3).
- » Design an "I have, who has?" activity using events from the novel. Include 20 cards (DOK 3).
- » Write an epilogue to the novel that examines how Petra and Calder are changed by their experience. Provide a justification connected to the character development throughout the novel (DOK 4).

LESSON 2.18

From the Mixed-Up Files of Mrs. Basil E. Frankweiler

CCSS ELA Standards

- » RL.8.2
- » RL.6.3
- » RL.7.3

Activities

- » Plan and perform the final scene of the book when Jamie and Claudia return home. Include a monologue introduction by either Jamie and Claudia's mother or father (DOK 1).
- » Create a poster announcing the showing of Angel at the museum. Include a picture of Angel, times, dates, place, and information on why people should attend (DOK 1).
- » Create a tournament of Jamie's favorite game: War. Include the game rules and the tournament bracket (DOK 2).
- » Create a profile, an explanation for why the novel should be read. Use a word associated with each aspect of the theme. Display creatively (DOK 2).
- » What happens when Claudia and Jamie return home? Write a final chapter to the novel that answers this question (DOK 3).
- » Create a book jacket, including illustrations, an enticing synopsis, author bio, and favorable reviews. Design a new book cover depicting the climax of the story. Write a newspaper book review article including important events from the book to persuade others to read it (DOK 3).
- » Design an "I have, who has?" activity using events from the novel. Include 20–30 cards. Have your class play the game. Afterwards, ask them to brainstorm additional questions and answers (DOK 3).
- » Write an epilogue to the novel that examines how Mrs. Basil E. Frankweiler is changed by her encounter with Jamie and Claudia. Consider including when the children meet her again with their grandfather. How does the author portray the changes that occur (DOK 4)?

LESSON 2.19
The Pushcart War

CCSS ELA Standards

- » RL.6.1
- » RL.6.2
- » RL.6.3

Activities

- » Create a map of New York City. Identify 10 key locations from the book. Locate each and give a brief explanation of the significance of each location (DOK 1).
- » Using specific and explicit events and details from the story, write an informational newspaper article reporting on the arrest of Harry the Hot Dog (DOK 2).
- » Create two Venn Diagrams or Double Bubble Maps. What do you see (DOK 2)?
  - ◆ Map 1: Compare pushcarts to trucks.
  - ◆ Map 2: Compare peddlers to truckers.

- » "Fortunately/Unfortunately . . . " Using this format, respond to an event in a selected chapter. Pay particular attention to sequencing and word choice (DOK 2).
- » Write a persuasive editorial from the point of view of the pushcart peddlers or the truckers. State your case and defend it by citing evidence from the text (DOK 3).
- » Design a pea tack shooter using the materials provided in the "shooter's bag." You will need a blueprint and working model (DOK 3).
- » Design a poster, T-shirt, or other artifact for a main character in the novel. Consider what makes this character compelling. Use the character's experiences, traits, and ideology to depict him or her in a clear, yet intriguing manner. Describe your intent and the rationale used in your design (DOK 3).
- » Select an event and character from the story with a perspective that can be contrasted with a similar event in another story. Critique the different perspectives relative to the stories (DOK 4).

LESSON 2.20
Walk Two Moons

CCSS ELA Standards

» RI.7.3
» RL.8.2
» RL.8.3

Activities

» Learn how the creation of monuments, such as Mount Rushmore, impacted the Native Americans in the area. What might have been some positive and negative attitudes they would have expressed had they been asked at the time of the monument's construction (DOK 2)?

» Examine how the roles of grandparents have changed over time in the United States, and how their roles differ in other countries, such as China. Suggest reasons for the changes (DOK 2).

» Research the origins, customs, location, and how the Seneca Indian tribe continues in present times. Describe ways in which their lifestyle has changed over time (DOK 3).

» Locate information related to geysers, such as Old Faithful in Yellowstone National Park. Find out how geysers work in general. Then create a hypothesis about the regularity of the eruption of Old Faithful. Compare your hypothesis with others' created by scientists over the years (DOK 3).

» Compare and contrast Sal and Phoebe's relationships with their mothers. Explore the traits these characters had in common with their parents and with each other (DOK 3).

» Identify and describe the locations that Sal and her grandparents encountered when they were searching for her mother. Imagine how those places would have appeared differently in Sal's time and in our current times. Create an ecological study describing the elements that may have caused those changes over time (DOK 3).

» Find several examples of the messages Phoebe received from the "lunatic." Decide how these messages hold special truths for Sal and Phoebe and how they learn important lessons. Connect your interpretation of what they mean to the events in the story (DOK 4).

» This book received the John Newbery Medal. Learn about the criteria used by those that bestow that award. Review other previous winners of this award to understand why they are deemed exceptional. What elements in this book do you believe influenced the judges to bestow that award (DOK 4)?

LESSON 2.21
The Phantom Tollbooth

CCSS ELA Standards

- » RL.6.2
- » RL.6.3

Activities

- » Write a script for a scene or chapter and/or perform a conversation between Milo and another character from the novel (DOK 1).
- » Examine the theme of *The Phantom Tollbooth*. Create a Wordle to express the idea of the theme (DOK 1).
- » Create a biography for one of the characters in *The Phantom Tollbooth* (DOK 2).
- » Characters in Dictionopolis are very fond of sayings and similes. Compile a booklet or digital presentation of sayings, proverbs, and similes that relate to the novel in some way. Include illustrations (DOK 2).
- » The Terrible Trivium gives Milo, Tock, and Humbug several pointless tasks to complete. Make an illustrated booklet (or digital presentation) of 10 other unimportant and time-consuming tasks he could have given his victims. Reference events from the book to show how these new tasks would fit the story (DOK 3).
- » Use a propaganda technique and include illustrations and text to create one of the following (DOK 3):
  - ◆ a travel brochure for an assigned land featured in *The Phantom Tollbooth*, or
  - ◆ a billboard that this land would display as you entered it.

- » Write an account of *The Phantom Tollbooth* from Tock's point of view (DOK 3).
- » Rewrite a chapter or scene in the book in a reader's theatre format. The selection must have a beginning, middle, and end to the scene. State your rationale for the version you created. Assemble a group of classmates to assist in performing the presentation (DOK 4).

3

Social Studies/History Extension Lessons

Introduction

Teachers who love teaching social studies and history enjoy having their students view what they are studying in myriad ways, such as through photographs, videos, websites, political cartoons, personal journals, timelines, and other media. To understand the significance of historical events, students must be able to decipher the implicit details found in varied text and visual formats. This helps them make meaning and develop understanding of the information. Students must also learn to provide support for their findings based on the explicit information provided.

Preassessment

The ability to move from the implicit to the explicit details is critical for developing students' understanding, especially in history because of the varied perspectives upon which history is recorded. Students need to learn how to make easily understandable that which is vague or implied from the onset. When studying history, students must learn to deconstruct events and information. Preassessment within this content can take many avenues. Standards often address specific components of the content that can be preassessed prior to moving students into a deeper conceptual understanding.

History is all about perspective. It is the ability to discern perspective from bias that enables the learner to make valid judgments regarding historical events. This describes the connection between the implicit and explicit detail recognition. Training students to look closely and critically at the material being studied and then make insightful connections is the role of the history teacher.

In the activities in this chapter, you will notice that we encourage the use of primary source documents. Using primary source documents requires students to use comprehension skills that allow them to read and examine text critically. When using primary source documents, students learn to discriminate between people's biases and perspectives to draw their own conclusions. They need to practice this type of careful analysis to determine and understand causal factors involved in the study of historical content.

The study of historical events allows students to delve into the deeper facets of understanding as they interact with the content. Students must do more than merely explain their thinking and provide examples. They must interpret information, apply principles, and view events through the varied lens of historical perspective. These higher order skills can be practiced and enhanced through activities in the extension lessons in this chapter.

Sample Lesson

In the sample lesson below, Mr. Perkins demonstrates how he incorporates the ELA standards into his history lesson. All students are participating in extension lesson activities in this scenario. In this particular lesson, compacting students out of the full unit could risk denying them the opportunity to delve more deeply into the content. As the unit progresses the teacher may identify aspects of the content in which particular students can demonstrate mastery. When this occurs, the students can be compacted out for the lesson and allowed to spend additional time on their extension lesson selections.

In this chapter's example, you will see Mr. Perkins using the "Conflict" extension lesson. Julia chose a Level 1 extension activity for her project. In this activity, she will study a period of revolution in two different countries. She will study the different viewpoints of the individuals impacted by the conflicts and identify the similarities and differences of these viewpoints.

Hakim selected a Level 3 extension activity. His level of understanding with regard to this topic is significantly more advanced than Julia's and therefore the level of depth and complexity of his task needs to match this understanding. The extension Hakim selected demands that he hypothesize what America's present-day life would be like if the "other side" had prevailed in a particular conflict in wartime. Hakim will need to determine how he will present his findings.

Students vary greatly in their conceptual understanding of historical events. Therefore, it is critical that extension lessons provide students with learning opportunities that address all of the Depth of Knowledge levels to ensure that students will have access to the varied degrees of complexity. Depending upon the specific content, a student may be working at different levels due to his or her prior exposure to the material.

Social Studies Example Lesson

Gifted students often have a strong sense of justice; many frequently view events as "right or wrong" or "black or white," and think there is no gray area. In this example lesson students are asked to view and read about multiple situations of conflict related to the Westward Expansion and the settlement of the United States. Students will learn through the process that oftentimes there is no "right or wrong." Students' conclusions will vary, yet all perspectives must include supporting evidence and/or rationale. As students work through this series of lessons they will be provided with the extension lesson, "Conflict." In this lesson, the choices presented require students to view events from multiple perspectives and consider diverse social and political issues. The teacher will guide students in exploring specific levels of depth and complexity levels within the extension lesson. Student performance on class activities and in Socratic discussion will provide the data used to determine the DOK level needed to provide appropriate challenge.

Essential Questions
5. What role did the U.S. Army play in western expansion and Native American removal?
6. How did visual images and newspaper accounts shape public opinion?
7. How were Native Americans impacted by ever-encroaching settlements?

Lesson Focus
Train students to become skilled visual viewers.

Objectives
Students will look thoughtfully at provided images, notice details, and infer how these details could shape a viewer's opinion. Students will closely read provided articles, notice details, and infer how these details could shape a viewer's opinion.

Standards
o   CCRA.R.1
o   CCRA.R.2
o   CCRA.R.3
o   CCRA.R.4

Key Vocabulary
Manifest Destiny, tableaux, visual image

Materials

Note. Multiple options can be found online.

o   Visual image: Indians Attack Settlers
o   News articles: Archived 1855–1870

Lesson Frame: Parts 1 and 2 (of a Six-Part Lesson)

Part 1: Students will divide a single sheet of paper into four sections. The visual image is projected onto the screen; students have several minutes to study the full image. They are instructed to frame the image into four sections and then view each section of the image individually. Students take notes on what they observe in the section in the corresponding square on the paper.

Pair/Share with table team: Students view the entire image again. With their table teammates students share what they observed in each section of the image. Students provide examples of how the details in each section of the image tell the story of the entire image. As a team, each group gives the story a title. Each team shares their title with the class along with their supporting evidence.

Closure: quick write. After listening to the titles shared by peers, direct students to choose the title they feel best represents this image and the message to be shared. They must then explain their thinking with supporting evidence.

Part 2: Within their table teams, provide students with several news articles relating to issues with the U.S. Army, settlers, and Native Americans between 1855 and 1863. Prior to reading the articles, students assume one of four roles army officer, settler, Native American, or government official. As students read the articles, they should read through the lens of their role.

Reading through the lens: Annotate your text. *What do you find important? What do you view as a problem? What do you view as outrageous? What do you feel is bias?*

Students will return to their table team to share and discuss the article. Students will compare how they reacted to the articles based on their role. Students select a portion of the article that they feel explains their reaction. Each student takes turns reading his or her selected passage out loud. Table teammates provide evidence that explains why they believe the section was chosen and how the student's role would have reacted. The student who selected the section initially will not share his or her thoughts until all tablemates have shared. When all students have shared, their reactions will be documented on large charts that are labeled with the roles.

The information students shared on their team charts will be discussed. Students will be asked to make connections between the news articles and the image shared previously.

Closure: Assign students to an opposing role (Native Americans vs. settlers). Write a journal reflection.

Extension Lesson

As students develop their reflection, the teacher will work individually to guide students to the DOK level of extension appropriate to meet their challenge needs. Students will be provided time to work on their extension lesson selection each day as the lesson series progresses. In this manner, students are provided with the additional challenge and an opportunity to extend their thinking.

LESSON 3.1
Ancient Civilizations

NCSS Standards

» I. Culture. a–d.

CCSS ELA Standards

» RH.6-8.1
» RH.6-8.7
» WHST.6-8.1
» WHST.6-8.8
» WHST.6-8.9

Activities

» Study and report on the geographic location and climatic events' impact on the history of the civilization you are studying (DOK 1).

» Create an eBay-type document advertising artifacts from an ancient civilization of your choice. Describe the use and importance of the items during that time (DOK 1).

» Study the religious or spiritual beliefs of this civilization, paying close attention to daily practices, superstitions, rituals, and practices regarding death and burial. Write an essay on the topic or create a chart showing your findings in which you provide an overview and include examples of how these beliefs are portrayed in daily life (DOK 2).

» Describe or demonstrate a technological advancement or invention of the time period studied. Trace its impact on current technology (DOK 2).

» Evaluate the contributions to present-day society from three different ancient civilizations. Order them in terms of their importance in modern use. Describe the criteria you used for the ranking (DOK 3).

» Describe the daily lives of people in different roles. Select several from the following groups: slaves, servants, shopkeepers, artisans, government leaders, religious practitioners, students in school, or other roles of your choosing. Report on the individuals' economic status relevant to the conditions in which they lived. Include a discussion on how the status of these roles would differ in today's world (DOK 4).

» Create a project in which you hypothesize about three potential causes of the fall or disappearance of this civilization. Analyze the degree to which each of these causes would be viable given the social, economic and/or political time (DOK 4).

» Compare the reign of one effective leader with one who was likely less favored by the common people. Find parallel examples in world leaders today. Consider and report on the possible characteristics that popular and unpopular leaders have in common throughout time (DOK 4).

LESSON 3.2
Middle Ages

NCSS Standards

» I. Culture. a–d

CCSS ELA Standards

» RH.6-8.1
» RH.6-8.7
» WHST.6-8.1
» WHST.6-8.2

Activities

» Study and report on the reasons why slavery was instituted as part of medieval life (DOK 1).
» Research the technology of the Middle Ages. Create a timeline of how technology progressed during this time period (DOK 1).
» Study various styles of dress throughout the Middle Ages. Determine the ways in which the dress helped or hindered daily life for the people in different roles or positions (DOK 2).
» Compare and contrast the economic structure of feudalism with that of capitalism. Provide real-life examples in your analysis (DOK 2).
» Choose a guild from this time period. Create a conversation among several of its members that highlights political, social, and/or economic problems they may have faced (DOK 3).
» Taking a holistic view regarding the times, consider various aspects of life, such as daily life, religious practices, warfare, governing styles, and a category of your choice. Explain a specific phenomena of the times, drawing upon several of the aspects noted here (DOK 3).
» Similar to the Bubonic Plague in the Middle Ages, epidemics still exist in the world today. Consider and discuss the differences in the diagnosis, treatment, and impact on people and society since the Middle Ages (DOK 3).
» Research different styles of castles. Evaluate the pros and cons of each in regard to safety, comfort, and conveniences. Create an improved design for one castle with these elements and the local environment in mind. Defend your rationale for your suggested changes (DOK 4).

LESSON 3.3
Feudalism and the Middle Ages

NCSS Standards

» I. Culture. a–d

CCSS ELA Standards

» RH.6-8.3
» RH.6-8.7
» RH.6-8.9
» WHST.6-8.4

Activities

» Illustrate and describe the costumes and dress of this time period for different groups of people: commoners, knights, royalty, entertainers, etc. (DOK 1).

» Select and read a biography of a king or queen who was powerful during this period. Read a play, poem or other piece of literature about the same monarch. Decide how closely the two literary pieces align. Support your assertions with evidence from the text (DOK 2).

» The Black Death (Bubonic plague) was rampant during the Middle Ages. Research the impact of the disease during this time. Include details describing the plague's infection, treatment, prevention, and survival aspects (DOK 2).

» The legends of King Arthur and the Knights of the Round Table continue to be of interest to people and performers. After studying several of these legends, consider the degree to which the stories were factual and/or fictional. In a presentation, share reasons why the stories have maintained their interest to people over time (DOK 3).

» Research the types of weapons used during sieges of castles or towns. Discuss the engineering and principles of physics involved in the making and use of the weapons. Include an assessment of the efficiency of their use for the time period (DOK 3).

» Research other countries that have used a feudalistic type of government structure sometime in their history. Compare and contrast the structures with those used in Europe during the Middle Ages (DOK 3).

» Read or view biographies of Richard the Lion-Hearted and Saladin. Create a format to interview the two leaders (DOK 4). In your discussion, include:
  ♦ their reasons for fighting the Third Crusade,
  ♦ their perspectives regarding the success or failure of their mission,
  ♦ their personal views regarding the current Middle East crises, and
  ♦ an analysis in which you critique their motives.

» Some of the diseases common in the Middle Ages, which seemed to have disappeared, may be making a comeback. The same virus that caused the Bubonic Plague may be plaguing us again. Gather information about these diseases and provide conjecture regarding the impact modern medicine may have (DOK 4).

LESSON 3.4
World War I and World War II

NCSS Standards

» VI. Power, Authority, & Governance: f, h

CCSS ELA Standards

» RH.6-8.7
» RH.6-8.9
» WHST.6-8.2

Activities

Activities in this extension lesson can be used for the study of either WWI or WWII.

» Interview people you know who have memories of life during the time period you are studying. Share your findings in a format of your choice (DOK 1).

» Create a project in which you illustrate some of the conditions people and nations face during times of world wars (DOK 1).

» Create a first-person narrative that illustrates the experience of someone who would have been directly involved in the conflict you are studying, from either the planning or action phases of the war (DOK 2).

» Study the use of propaganda by both sides in one of the world wars. Identify similarities and differences used by both sides and evaluate the effectiveness of the propaganda (DOK 2).

» Research war protest movements over time. Report on the similarities and differences between protest tactics and results in different eras of American history. Identify trends and hypothesize as to future direction (DOK 3).

» Examine the methods of diplomacy of the U.S. during each world war. Describe your interpretation of the successes and failures of diplomatic measures during times of world war (DOK 3).

» Examine ways in which the music of the time reflected the events taking place. Develop a logical argument explaining how music helped or hindered people's emotions and living conditions for both civilians and military personnel (DOK 4).

» Examine and report on the ethical considerations of using weapons of mass destruction. Include a response to the assertion that using such weapons could ultimately save lives of soldiers and civilians if the weaponry resulted in the conflict ending sooner (DOK 4).

LESSON 3.5

The Holocaust

NCSS Standards

» IX. Global Connections: a–f

CCSS ELA Standards

» RH.6-8.4
» WHST.6-8.1
» WHST.6-8.8
» WHST.6-8.9

Activities

» Define "holocaust." Given this definition, identify examples of holocaust situations throughout history (DOK 1).
» Identify and report on agencies around the world that are devoted to protecting human rights. Explain how their efforts are connected to holocaust practices over time (DOK 2).
» Prisoner of War situations have similarities to holocaust situations. Explore and report the decades for both foreign and domestic locations (DOK 2).
» Explore the situation of the Japanese internment camps in the United States during World War II. Determine the extent to which this situation was similar to and different from the Holocaust happening in Europe during the same time period (DOK 2).
» A clash of religious beliefs is often an integral part of a holocaust. Investigate three such clashes since 2000 and determine the degree to which the situation might have qualified as a holocaust (DOK 3).
» Hypothesize as to the reasons why victims of holocausts did not resist the forces that were growing against them or foment an uprising. Compare these reasons to events in which such an uprising did occur (DOK 3).
» When people think "holocaust," they generally associate it with the Nazi atrocities of World War II. Investigate two other periods in history that could be considered a holocaust. Determine the similarities and differences of the situations in those periods to the Holocaust of World War II (DOK 4).

» Keeping information about historical holocausts alive is part of a process of helping people understand why holocausts should never occur again. However, even today we can find evidence of holocausts in some parts of the world. Investigate contemporary holocaust situations and draw conclusions as to why the world is unable to eradicate them. Create suggestions that might reverse such situations (DOK 4).

LESSON 3.6
Explorers of the New World

NCSS Standards

» VI. Power, Authority, & Governance: f–h
» IX. Global Connections: a, b

CCSS ELA Standards

» RH.6-8.3
» RH.6-8.7
» WHST.6-8.1
» WHST.6-8.6
» WHST.6-8.8
» WHST.6-8.9

Activities

» Make a list that identifies the explorers who "discovered" America. Reference their contributions and their impact on the Native Americans they encountered (DOK 1).

» Create an illustrated digital storybook of an explorer. Discuss the "who, what, when, where, and why" of his or her contributions to the discovery of the New World. Include references (DOK 1).

» Design a graphic display of explorers who "discovered" America and identify patterns and similarities (DOK 2).

» Create a "Cause and Effect" presentation of the impact the explorers had on the Native American civilizations in the New World (DOK 2).

» Make a logbook that provides a literary account of what the explorers went through to reach the new land and adapt to the many challenges they faced. Reference topics such as: what was on board the ships, storms at sea, parts of the ocean that were particularly dangerous, disease, scarcity of provisions, and/or other challenging situations the explorers faced. Include details describing the length of the trip using specific dates and information gleaned from your research (DOK 2).

» Create a log describing the contributions of European explorers who discovered America. Consider including photos, maps, and/or videos. Add fictional events that may have transpired with the explorers and their crew and hypothesize as to their reflections on the journey given the difficulties they faced. Cite evidence and include references (DOK 3).

» Write a journal that includes entries from the perspective of a young sailor or cabin boy who was on the journey to the New World. Explore his point of view about encountering the new land and the interactions with native tribes that were friendly and unfriendly. Synthesize information collected from actual accounts and include them as reference material to ascertain an accurate portrayal. Include references (DOK 4).

» Reflect upon the reasons why the explorers of the New World made their journeys. Compare these reasons to other explorers of "new worlds." Identify themes (such as seeking religious freedom, trade routes, and resources) that each group shared. Discuss the explorers' motivations, support systems, and challenges within these themes (DOK 4).

LESSON 3.7
Exploration and Explorers

NCSS Standards

» VI. Power, Authority, & Governance: f–h
» IX. Global Connections: a, b

CCSS ELA Standards

» RH.6-8.1
» RH.6-8.9
» WHST.6-8.8
» WHST.6-8.9

Activities

» In a region currently being studied in your class, research the effects of exploration on the indigenous people who lived in the explored areas. Create a chart describing both positive and negative impacts on the indigenous people in that area (DOK 1).

» Examine two to three accounts of a specific exploration, such as that of Lewis and Clark. Describe differences between the accounts. Draw conclusions about which version(s) may be closer to the truth and provide rationale for your conclusions. Include references (DOK 2).

» Consider the explorations of astronauts and those who explore under the sea. Create a project that describes the similarities and difference between these endeavors (DOK 2).

» Analyze how some skills needed by Old World explorers hundreds of years ago apply to those of 21st-century explorers (DOK 3).

» There have been some attempts to discredit the discoveries of explorers, such as Christopher Columbus. Identify one explorer and investigate reasons for these campaigns, drawing your own conclusions about the debate. Include evidence to support your conclusions (DOK 3).

» Consider how America would be different today if the British had not come to America. Based on contributions they made, speculate as to how life would have been different. Create a presentation depicting this scenario in the United States. Describe possible global ramifications in these situations (DOK 4).

» Study a topic in science being explored today. Trace this topic back through history and examine the differences in exploration techniques of this topic throughout history. Consider how political and societal times influence exploration techniques (DOK 4).

» Critique the work and goals of several 19th- and 20th-century explorers and missionaries in terms of their impact on the people they "discovered" and with whom they interacted. In your discussion, include and analyze resulting outcomes of these individuals' work (DOK 4).

LESSON 3.8

Puritan Colonization of the New World

NCSS Standards

- » III. People, Places, & Environments: h
- » V. Individuals, Groups, & Institutions: b

CCSS ELA Standards

- » RH.6-8.1
- » RH.6-8.9
- » WHST.6-8.4

Activities

- » Study and present on the realities of the ocean voyage these settlers endured, including food, sleeping, personal hygiene, fears, illness, and other challenges (DOK 1).
- » Imagine and report on a day in the life of a Puritan or Pilgrim youngster. Include information about clothes, chores, games, education, fears, and/or other elements (DOK 1).
- » Examine the role of women in the early colonies. Investigate and report on the efforts of certain women to change these realities (DOK 2).
- » Study the design of a typical colonial village or town. Create a digital replica and describe the rationale for the design (DOK 2).
- » Evaluate the rationale behind the attempts to legalize slavery in the colonies for the purpose of promoting economic growth in the New World (DOK 3).
- » Compare and contrast the Puritans and Pilgrims. Take into account their lifestyles, religious and political beliefs, and their reasons for coming to the New World (DOK 3).
- » Examine the reasons and motivations for England to colonize the New World. Decide why those motivations would or would not have been valid today. Look for events based on similar motivations that have transpired since. Synthesize your findings in a presentation (DOK 4).

» Study the colonists' efforts to achieve religious freedom and contrast that evidence with ways in which colonists interfered with religious freedom for some of their neighbors (DOK 4).

LESSON 3.9
Colonies in the New World

NCSS Standards

» III. People, Places, & Environments: h
» V. Individuals, Groups, & Institutions: b

CCSS ELA Standards

» RH.6-8.1
» RH.6-8.7
» WHST.6-8.1
» WHST.6-8.4

Activities

» Construct a three-dimensional map of one of the settlements. Include the layout of the colony in your replica and a labeled explanation of each building and its use to the colony for its survival (DOK 1).

» Create a timeline depicting colonization from the establishment of Jamestown through the 1750s. Provide illustrations for some of your selected events (DOK 1).

» Research the first Thanksgiving. Make a "Fact Versus Fiction" chart. List beliefs about the event that are true and those that have been proven false or for which we are simply unsure of their accuracy (DOK 2).

» Create a Venn diagram to compare and contrast the New England, Middle, and Southern Colonies. What conclusions can you draw from your diagram (DOK 2)?

» Write a newspaper article for a colonial newspaper chronicling a significant event during this time period. Research it carefully to provide an accurate account and use the language of the time (DOK 3).

» Choose three colonies. Write a comparative analysis and create a depiction explaining how the location of the colony, its society, and its government either helped or hindered its survival (DOK 3).

» Locate three websites that provide information about the colonization of America. After studying each, analyze the consistency and validity of the information presented on the three sites (DOK 4).

» Create a map of the geography of three of the settlements. Include annotations that discuss the geography of the area and label the appropriate bodies of water. Drawing from multiple sources, provide an explanation as to why the settlers chose that location. Consider whether the location helped or hindered the colonies throughout different times. Include both real examples and conjectures to support your conclusion (DOK 4).

LESSON 3.10
Challenges in the New World

NCSS Standards

» III. People, Places, & Environments: h
» V. Individuals, Groups, & Institutions: b

CCSS ELA Standards

» RH.6-8.1
» RH.6-8.7
» WHST.6-8.1
» WHST.6-8.4

Activities

» Draw a map of the New World in 1750. Label colonies and other land areas in North America (DOK 1).

» Research common diseases in the New World during the 1700s. Make a chart listing several diseases and the medication and treatments used with these diseases. Provide evidence of the mortality rate for early settlers affected by these diseases (DOK 2).

» Create a colonial fashion magazine depicting the fashions for early colonists, both male and female. Include advertisements that the readership would find interesting and valuable. Include true costs of the garments (DOK 2).

» Research the dietary options available to the colonists. Create a 5-day menu to meet their dietary needs (DOK 2).

» Make a speech convincing your neighbors in England NOT to travel and settle in the New World. Include real dangers and myths people may have believed at the time, as well as possible living situations they may encounter in the New World. Present your speech to class (DOK 3).

» Design an advertisement or poster to convince people to make the voyage to the New World. Include reasons for making the journey, transportation options, and information regarding settlements and future opportunities (DOK 3).

» Create a digital illustration depicting interaction and dialogue between two of the following: a colonial child, a settler, and/or a storekeeper. The dialogue should describe an important topic or debate of the time. Include references (DOK 4).

» Write two sets of diary entries describing the arrival of a group of settlers from the points of view of two of the following: a newly arrived settler, an established settler, and/or an Indian. Include pertinent issues of the time from the selected individuals' perspective (DOK 4).

LESSON 3.11
John Smith and the 13 Colonies

NCSS Standards

- » III. People, Places, & Environments: h
- » V. Individuals, Groups, & Institutions: b

CCSS ELA Standards

- » RH.6-8.1
- » WHST.6-8.1
- » WHST.6-8.8
- » WHST.6-8.9

Activities

- » Make a scrapbook or digital presentation featuring 10 historical figures from this time period (DOK 1).
- » Draw a map of the 13 colonies and label at least five cities where important events took place. Describe the events (DOK 1).
- » Make a timeline of the major events in the textbook that pertain to the 13 colonies and John Smith. Describe the importance of the events (DOK 2).
- » Write a series of diary entries as if you were Pocahontas planning to say good-bye to your good friend, John Smith (DOK 2).
- » Read *The Starving Time*. Then find another account of the same topic and similar theme depicting this same time and location. Contrast and compare the two stories (DOK 2).
- » Write an essay discussing which colony you would have liked to live in and explain why you chose this colony. Include details and life activities in your colony of choice to support your choice. Cite references to support your decisions (DOK 3).
- » Write an opinion piece about whether you agree or disagree with John Smith's "Don't work; don't eat" rule (DOK 3).
- » Make a triple Venn diagram comparing and contrasting the social, political, and economic times in the New England, Middle, and Southern Colonies. Critique your findings by analyzing the similarities and differences in the context of the times (DOK 4).

LESSON 3.12
American Revolution and the Stamp Act

NCSS Standards

» II, Time, Continuity, & Change: a–d

CCSS ELA Standards

» RH.6-8.3
» RH.6-8.7
» WHST.6-8.1
» WHST.6-8.2

Activities

» Write a news brief for a colonial newspaper describing the situation in Boston because the harbor closing. Include a graphic and cite your sources (DOK 1).
» Pretend you are a colonist. Write a letter to a friend and list items that you want or need in your daily life that will likely be impacted by the Stamp Act (DOK 1).
» Write and illustrate a storybook depicting and explaining the who, what, where, when, and why of either the Stamp Act or the Boston Tea Party. If digital, include a video clip from a reliable source (DOK 2).
» Write a newspaper article describing how the harbor's closing is affecting the city and changing people's attitudes (DOK 2).
» Assume the role of a colonist and write a letter to the prime minister describing how the daily lives of the colonists will suffer as a result of the Stamp Act. Formulate ideas for alternative actions that might result in less turmoil for the colonists (DOK 3).
» Compare and contrast the views of the Loyalists with those of the Patriots. Formulate an editorial perspective that you support by citing evidence (DOK 3).
» As prime minister, write a letter to the colonists discussing the potential financial benefits to the government resulting from the Stamp Act. Attempt

to convince the colonists why the government needs additional income and why the act is fair (DOK 4).

» Write a short story of historical fiction choosing the perspective of either a Loyalist or a Patriot. Add events that lead to the American Revolution, including those from the Boston Tea Party and the Stamp Act. Provide all information from the point of view of a chosen character. At the same time, relate the possible repercussions of the events for both sides (DOK 4).

LESSON 3.13
American Revolution: Causal Factors

NCSS Standards

» VI. Power, Authority, & Governance: f, h

CCSS ELA Standards

» RH.6-8.1
» RH.6-8.7
» WHST.6-8.1
» WHST.6-8.4

Activities

» Create a timeline in which you identify the events that led to the American Revolution. Include dates, names, locations, and any other pertinent information you find in your research (DOK 1).

» Write a week's worth of journal entries from a child's point of view during the American Revolution. The entries should reflect on what is happening as a result of the conflict (DOK 2).

» Create a Jeopardy game for the Revolution using the headings: dates, places, people, causes, and battles (DOK 2).

» With a partner, debate whether the colonies should separate from British rule. Each person must take an opposing stance. Together, create a presentation defending your stance. Cite evidence as support (DOK 2).

» It is impossible to know the exact number of American colonists who favored or opposed independence. Compare and contrast the Loyalists and the Patriots' viewpoints. Select one group and develop a convincing argument for siding with that group (DOK 3).

» View several videos of "The Star-Spangled Banner" from educationally respected websites, such as the History Channel, Smithsonian Institute, or *History Detectives* on PBS, etc. Identify what depictions are more and less prevalent among the sites' videos. Describe how the videos differ. Draw conclusions as to why the different organizations might highlight different aspects of our national anthem (DOK 4).

» Look at descriptions of TV shows and movies made about the Revolutionary War. Select two or three of your favorites. Analyze the degree to which they accurately reflect life during the war. Identify one major controversy pertaining to the war. Critique how these depictions address this controversy (DOK 4).

» Design an advertisement to recruit more soldiers for the war. Appeal to events occurring during the time to convince people that they owe it to the nation to enlist. Support your assertions by citing evidence of real events (DOK 4).

LESSON 3.14
Civil War

CCSS ELA Standards

- » RH.6-8.1
- » RH.6-8.7
- » WHST.6-8.1
- » WHST.6-8.4

Activities

- » Construct a timeline of key events and battles of the Civil War (DOK 1).
- » Plan a Civil War reenactment of any battle (DOK 2).
- » Draw a blueprint of the inside of a tent or barrack of a Civil War soldier (DOK 2).
- » Write a menu for breakfast, lunch, and dinner that would have been served to a Civil War military unit (DOK 2).
- » Create an infographic in which you demonstrate how the Civil War changed the history of the United States (DOK 3).
- » Research songs and instruments used during the time period of the Civil War. Describe these and then identify a favorite song and instrument to discuss in more detail. Examine the song's relevance to the times (DOK 3).
- » Pretend you are a tour guide of Gettysburg. Explain what you would see on the tour and what you would say as the guide. Consider what topics you might be reluctant to discuss if you were the actual tour guide and the reasons for your reluctance (DOK 3).
- » Use primary sources to examine how news was reported during the Civil War. Write a critique of the news reporting given what you know about the outcome of the war (DOK 4).

LESSON 3.15
American Wars

NCSS Standards

» VI. Power, Authority, & Governance: f, h

CCSS ELA Standards

» RH.6-8.3
» RH.6-8.7
» WHST.6-8.1
» WHST.6-8.2

Activities

» Choose 25 key words from this unit. Create a directory that lists each word, its meaning, and its relevance to this war (DOK 1).

» Locate information about the medical practices used on the battlefield and in field hospitals during this war. Describe your findings in a report. Include biographical information about famous medical people of that time (DOK 1).

» Present a detailed biography of an important person during the time of this conflict. Include evidence of this person's influence during the war period (DOK 2).

» Research the patriotic music used by both sides of the war. Point out similarities and differences. Describe how music influences patriotism in civilians and soldiers (DOK 2).

» Learn about the ways in which those in the military communicated with each other and with their commander-in-chief during this war. Focus on events in which poorly delivered communication influenced the outcome of a military effort. Present your findings (DOK 3).

» Investigate battles in which creative or uncommonly used tactics for the time were employed. Report on the success of these creative tactics. Design strategies that you think would have led to more victories and fewer casualties. Incorporate only the technology available during that time period (DOK 3).

» Research other types of wars: between families, clans, and/or those involving mythical creatures, superheroes etc. Share information about them and describe comparisons of elements found in an American war (DOK 4).

» Are there alternatives to war? Select several conflicts that have resulted in war. What obstacles were encountered in the peacekeeping process? Consider how these obstacles may have prevented alternative methods from being successful. Take a stand and defend your position: Is war preventable (DOK 4)?

LESSON 3.16
Study of a Decade

NCSS Standards

> » II. Time, Continuity, & Change: a–e

CCSS ELA Standards

> » RH.6-8.1
> » RH.6-8.9
> » WHST.6-8.8
> » WHST.6-8.9

Activities

> » Study the demographics of the decade. Report on the reasons for the movement or lack of movement of people during that time (DOK 1).

> » Study the characteristics of "peaceful" versus "violent" decades. Create an explanation of the factors that existed that made the decade become characterized by these categories (DOK 2).

> » Choose a hot political topic of the decade and design a campaign to either pass or defeat a law about it (DOK 2).

> » Identify who you feel to be the five most important people of a particular decade. Rank order them and support your rankings by citing evidence (DOK 3).

> » Identify and describe a political, economic, or social effort of the decade that has had a lasting impact in today's world. Describe its continuing impact. Hypothesize as to how history would have changed if the event had not taken place (DOK 3).

> » Historians often refer to decades by the names of the prevailing trends of the time. Investigate how this process works and hypothesize as to how you or your children's generation might be remembered. Support your hypothesis by referencing past, current, and emerging trends (DOK 4).

> » Throughout history, nations struggle with the issue of being challenged by another political system, such as socialism or communism. Analyze similarities and differences concerning this issue during different decades of American

history. Identify trends and draw conclusions to discuss in conjunction with your findings (DOK 4).

» Examine famous legal cases of the decade. Determine the extent to which the cases might have turned out the same or differently if they had occurred in present times (DOK 4).

LESSON 3.17

World Cultures

NCSS Standards

» Culture: a, c

CCSS ELA Standards

» RH.6-8.4
» RH.6-8.9
» WHST.6-8.7
» WHST.6-8.8
» WHST.6-8.9

Activities

» Choose 15–20 keywords that relate to the culture of the country you are studying. Create a presentation in which you define and depict the word in a graphic display of your choosing (DOK 1).

» Examine the culture of the people from a particular country you are studying to discover how their country's geography impacts their lives (DOK 2).

» Select and study at least three myths, legends, and/or folk tales that come from the culture you are studying. Identify the moral or theme of each story. Compare and contrast these themes (DOK 3).

» Identify and examine several typical musical instruments from the culture you are studying. Create a presentation in which you describe how the sounds and movements reflect the values of this culture (DOK 3).

» Identify and elaborate upon a technological achievement from the culture being studied and assess its effects on the society in current times (DOK 3).

» Research the religious, spiritual, or cultural beliefs of this culture and trace the origins of those beliefs into the history of this culture, going back to the ancient civilizations that were dominant in this part of the world (DOK 3).

» Closely examine an issue that was of current interest to the culture you are studying. Identify the issue's original causes and consider ways in which the issue might be solved given current conditions in this culture and the world at large. Discuss its relevance to the culture where you live (DOK 4).

» Research both a former political and a religious leader from the culture you are studying. Report on these individuals' similarities and differences when compared to current leaders in the same cultures. Analyze these individuals' impact on current leaders (DOK 4).

LESSON 3.18
Teens in Other Cultures

NCSS Standards

» IX. Global Connections: a–f

CCSS ELA Standards

» RH.6-8.1
» RH.6-8.2
» RH.6-8.8
» RH.6-8.9

Activities

» Research life as a teenager in another country. Describe the rituals they must experience in order to make the transition to adulthood (DOK 1).
» Describe 10–20 details about the daily lives of teens in the country you are studying or a country of your choice (DOK 1).
» Within a specific culture, investigate whether all teens experience similar coming of age rituals, or if the rituals differ according to the social class or status of different teens. Create a graphic display that showcases these rituals and allows us to examine their similarities and differences (DOK 2).
» Learn about how the lives of teens have changed in a country of your choosing during the last several decades. Create a visual timeline representing this pattern (DOK 2).
» Compare and contrast your own educational experience as a teen with the educational experience of a teen in the country you are studying. Draw conclusions as to how the social, cultural, or political norms impact the teens' education (DOK 3).
» Interview a person over age 65. Compare and contrast the similarities and differences of being a teenager then and now. Describe the differences within the context of the times. Identify strengths or advantages of both time periods (DOK 3).
» Based on your own experience as a teen, develop a theory on how to teach teenage students. Use anecdotal evidence from your own life, the experiences of others, or primary sources of documentation (DOK 4).

» Investigate and report on the experience of being a teen in countries where children marry at a young age. Develop an argument that explains why these practices prevail in these cultures. Include a discussion on our culture's opposing point of view and why it is not a practice we use (DOK 4).

LESSON 3.19
Discovery and Colonization

NCSS Standards

» III. People, Places, & Environments: h
» V.Individuals, Groups, & Institutions: b

CCSS ELA Standards

» RH.6-8.1
» RH.6-8.7
» WHST.6-8.9

Activities

» Create a series of diary entries of a famous explorer. Include observations, daily life events, dangers, and surprises. Cite references (DOK 1).
» Design a mural depicting several aspects of life in a specific colony. Reference the assertions you depict in your illustration (DOK 2).
» Research the debate in the United States over celebrating Columbus Day. Record your findings. Include your opinion on the matter (DOK 2).
» Create a newspaper from a time in history when colonization was taking place. Include features on topics such as food, entertainment, political debates, education, medical issues, dangers, etc. (DOK 3).
» Some people fear there is nothing left for humans to "explore." Create a list of places still in need of exploration. Order them in the order of importance. Provide an explanation for your rankings (DOK 3).
» There are positive and negative aspects of exploration and colonization. Investigate these conflicting aspects and describe examples of both. Support your reasoning by citing respected references (DOK 3).
» Examine the history of space exploration. Make a case regarding its economic feasibility and rationalize your position. In your discussion, include political, legal, ethical, and/or other considerations involved in continuing to develop or as reasons to discontinue space programs (DOK 4).
» Discovery often seems to imply a sense of ownership. Identify and discuss issues related to the discovery of a region and the impact on current inhabitants. Do we "own" what we discover? Provide examples from both past and current instances in your presentation (DOK 4).

LESSON 3.20
Iditarod

NCSS Standards

» IV. Individual Development & Identity: a, b, d, g

CCSS ELA Standards

» RH.6-8.1
» WHST.6-8.1
» WHST.6-8.8
» WHST.6-8.9

Activities

Note. The Iditarod is a long-distance endurance race with dogsleds in Alaska.

» Research and compile a list of problems encountered by drivers in other Iditarod races (DOK 1).
» Create an advertisement designed to entice people to participate in the next Iditarod (DOK 2).
» You are the driver in an upcoming race. Research common problems encountered by drivers in previous races. Anticipate the problems you might encounter given the circumstances and develop potential solutions (DOK 2).
» Imagine being a driver in a race. Create a project that describes your physical surroundings during this trip. Predict how the surroundings impact the driver and the team of dogs (DOK 2).
» Research the origins of the Iditarod. Consider and discuss how the race emerged within the historical context of the time (DOK 3).
» You have fallen asleep on your sled and awake to find your dogs all tangled. You are unsure of your location. Describe the life skills you will utilize to remedy this situation. Consider how you might prepare for this in advance (DOK 3).
» There are a number of simulations that offer students the opportunity to obtain the Iditarod experience. Research the key aspects of the race and identify the elements that are most crucial in understanding the race itself. Then research two simulations and evaluate their effectiveness in providing a real-

istic Iditarod experience. Develop a matrix sharing your results and recommendations (DOK 4).

» Although your team is fed, rested, and bootied and have been pulling well, you are totally exhausted. Create a plan to refresh yourself physically and psychologically. Include attention to perseverance (DOK 4).

LESSON 3.21
Native American Life

NCSS Standards

» V. Individuals, Groups, & Institutions: b
» VI. Power, Authority, & Governance: a
» IX. Global Connections: b

CCSS ELA Standards

» RH.6-8.1
» RH.9-10.9
» WHST.6-8.7
» WHST.6-8.8

Activities

» Identify the Native American tribes that have occupied the region in which you live. Describe each, noting the time periods, locations, and specifics pertaining to the lives of the people (DOK 1).
» Compare and contrast elements found in myths and legends from three groups of Native Americans: one from your region and two from other regions. List the elements they have in common and those that are endemic to only one of the three tribes (DOK 2).
» Study the life story of an important Native American leader in the 1800s. Describe his or her leadership role and contributions to their cultural groups (DOK 2).
» Examine the degree to which ancient customs are still practiced by members of a tribe that lives in your state. View videos of gatherings in which these customs are demonstrated. Create a project describing what you have learned (DOK 2).
» Conduct research on the living conditions on Native American reservations before the advent of income from casinos. Describe ways in which life on these reservations has changed. Formulate an opinion as to the degree that the changes have improved or harmed the tribes' cultures (DOK 3).
» Native Americans represent one group of Americans that have unusually high rates of alcoholism among its members. Construct a hypothesis to determine

the reasons for this problem. Describe methods that have been employed to address the concern (DOK 3).

» Examine the connections between nature and religion for Native Americans. Discuss how the dramatic changes in the people's way of life from the 1600s to the present have impacted these connections (DOK 4).

» Examine and report on the emergence of casinos around the country and how they have influenced the economic well-being of Native Americans. In your discussion, include and defend your position on the issue of whether these casinos should pay taxes to the state or federal governments (DOK 4).

LESSON 3.22
Economics

NCSS Standards

» VII. Production, Distribution, & Consumption: a–i

CCSS ELA Standards

» RH.6-8.1
» RH.6-8.9
» WHST.6-8.7
» WHST.6-8.8
» WHST.6-8.9

Activities

» Identify goods and services (e.g., fire and police protection, immunizations, library) provided by local governments. Discuss what could happen if the government did not provide them. Share your ideas through a project format of your choosing (DOK 1).

» Research a city of interest anywhere in the world and create an advertisement promoting its economy to entice people to move there for economic reasons (DOK 2).

» Research various levels of professions in terms of expected salary. Select one current job opportunity from each level you define. Discuss the rationale for the different salary levels and describe the differences in costs of living for the levels (DOK 2).

» Research examples of trade in your local community or state (e.g., farmers supply the grocer). Create a project to show what you have found. Include your recommendations on how to improve trade in the community (DOK 3).

» Choose a geographical area and investigate how scarcity requires people to make choices due to their wants and needs. Forecast what you see happening in the future for this area. Describe possible economic outcomes (DOK 3).

» Investigate reasons (e.g., labor, raw materials, energy resources) as to why some goods are made and sold locally and some are made and sold in other parts of the United States and world. Consider economic benefits and disadvantages for local and foreign made products. Explain your findings through a presentation (DOK 3).

» Create a simulation game showing the benefits and disadvantages of personal spending and saving choices during differing periods of economic growth (DOK 4).

» Consider the economic goals of different groups and institutions, such as families, workers, banks, labor unions, government agencies, small businesses, and large corporations. Create a project wherein you relate the economic goals of some of these to political relationships and affiliations. Include a discussion and examples of how politics influences economic decisions by the different groups (DOK 4).

LESSON 3.23
Government

NCSS Standards

» VI. Power, Authority, & Governance: b–e

CCSS ELA Standards

» RH.6-8.7
» RH.6-8.9
» WHST.6-8.7
» WHST.6-8.8
» WHST.6-8.9

Activities

» Describe the electoral system used in the United States voting process and reasons why it was put into place. List strengths and weaknesses of this system (DOK 1).

» Prepare a biography of a person who served our federal government at any time in our history. Include a discussion on this person's legacy following his or her time in office (DOK 2).

» Study an event in American history during which time the rights of individuals were sacrificed in the interest of national security, such as the internment of Japanese citizens during World War II and of people of Arab background after September 11, 2001. Summarize the politics of such actions (DOK 2).

» Research the presence of federalism in our history. Categorize which powers overlap between state and federal governments and hypothesize as to the effects of practices that lean too far either way (DOK 3).

» Research several forms of government such as dictatorship, communism, socialism, oligarchy, theocracy, monarchy, parliamentary democracies, and/or autocracy. Provide examples of countries that utilize each form you choose. Evaluate the strengths and weaknesses of each of these and make a case for either maintaining or changing the form of government for a given country (DOK 3).

» Politicians have been challenged to find ways to convince younger people to become more active voters. Design a campaign to make this happen (DOK 3).

» Hypothesize as to how life in America would be different if the phrase from the Declaration of Independence, "All men are created equal . . . " was initially followed to the extent of its intent. Identify important aspects of our lives that would be different under this scenario (DOK 4).

» Identify, examine, and critique policies that some believe might be in conflict with the Constitution (DOK 4).

4

Mathematics Extension Lessons

Introduction

The leveled activities in this section offer students the opportunity for productive struggle. As discussed in Chapter 1, opportunity to engage in productive struggle is vital for the learning process, and for high-ability students, this opportunity involves moving beyond traditional curriculum options. Through the use of extension lessons in mathematics, students learn to persevere through challenging tasks within which they may have had limited or even extensive exposure. The basic mathematical constructs are in place, but the tasks require students to seek options beyond those that may come readily to mind.

Preassessment

Many teachers feel that mathematics is the easiest discipline in which to provide preassessment data. However, the idea that the student can either do the computation or cannot leaves out a valuable component in the learning process. Computational understanding does not ensure conceptual understanding. Teachers commonly find students with algorithmic knowledge that exceed their conceptual understandings. It is critical that the tool used to develop a preassessment requires the student to demonstrate conceptual understanding commensurate with the algorithmic computational understanding being demonstrated.

Connections to Standards

Mathematics is a problem-solving-based domain, a critical component of the Common Core State Standards for Mathematics (CCSS-M; NGA & CCSSO, 2010b). Teachers are now tasked with moving beyond traditionally honored procedures wherein algorithms are modeled, practiced, and tested, and then instruction moves on to the next standard or concept. The Mathematical Practices, foundational elements of the CCSS-M, demand a level of understanding beyond learning an algorithm. Supporting students in developing an understanding of *why* the algorithm works and what other means can be used to solve the problem become fundamental in the teaching and learning process.

The Mathematical Practices prepare students to engage with problems that they have not previously been taught, a process that reflects what students are required to do on performance-based assessments. By design, performance-based assessments engage students in problems that require a demonstration of the conceptual understanding. The problems require the student to use previous knowledge, and abstract thinking to determine solutions even though the problem itself has not been previously encountered. The extension lessons here, including the sample lesson, help prepare students for this type of performance-based problem solving.

Connections to DOK Levels

Exploring the four Depth of Knowledge levels in mathematics requires a different lens than when using them in the other content areas. As noted, mathematics is often seen as an algorithm driven content area. By viewing the content through the lenses of the Mathematical Practices and the DOK levels, we learn that the process of understanding mathematics is concept driven rather than algorithm driven.

The DOK-leveled activities in mathematics look slightly different than in the other content areas, due to the linear development of mathematical concepts. The following descriptions demonstrate the differences between the levels and the ways in which students can progress through the levels to obtain deeper conceptual understandings. At Recall, or DOK Level 1, the student must recall information to perform a simple procedure or operation. This is an example of one-step mathematics, well defined and straightforward. At this level, the student demonstrates a rote process, follows a well-practiced algorithm, or completes a defined set of steps.

The move to Level 2 begins when the students are asked to determine "how" to solve the problem presented. These are not single step activities. For example, they may require the student to make observations, to organize information, or to estimate. Students working in Level 2 might be asked to interpret information found in a simple graphic. They need to classify, organize, compare, and display data in a basic graphic format.

As students move into learning activities in Level 3, the degree of abstraction increases, as do the cognitive demands. The demands at this level are clearly more complex. The increase in complexity comes from the levels of reasoning and problem solving required by the student. Whereas Level 2 problems require straightforward solutions, most often Level 3 problems demand justification and critical thinking that can be evidenced through a variety of formats. Students working at this level will make conjectures based on the information in the problem as part of the solution process.

The step to Level 4 can be found in the application of conceptual understanding through creative and critical thinking skills. At this level, the cognitive demand is intense and the tasks are complex. This complexity requires students to interpret and break through the complexity of the math problem. They need to figure out what is being asked in order to consider various solution options and then select one approach as to how the situation could be solved. Level 4 mathematics activities represent real-world relevancy. Students will need to make connections, relate ideas among various content areas, and draw upon past knowledge. They then must connect and synthesize the information in order to create new and novel understandings within the context of the problem being solved.

To fully address the learning needs of today's middle school math students, the DOK levels must be viewed in conjunction with the Mathematical Practices. The DOK levels engage the student in complex problems that require the fluent use of the Practices. The Practices provide the vehicle by which students will solve the problems. When designing activities within the extension lessons, attempt to provide activities that address the range of Mathematical Practices to ensure that students are being exposed to all of the practices rather than a select few.

Conversion to the CCSS means that today's math students will need more than a list of algorithms that allow them to plug in information to known formulas. They must be able to discern what is needed to solve complex problems for which no algorithm has been developed. Placing students in learning situations that promote appropriate challenge allows them to develop the Mathematical Practice frameworks they will need to succeed in the future math endeavors. The extension lessons in this chapter are designed for this purpose.

Sample Lesson

Providing students with the need-to-know experience is critical when engaging them in the mathematical process. In this sample lesson, students are encouraged to explore a variety of elements and variables in finding a perfect solution. Their understandings will be demonstrated through the exploration process. This lesson allows for more than one viable solution; it remains the challenge for the student to provide the justification needed for the solution selected. As students work through the lesson, multiple standards and strategies are incorporated. One value of need-to-know exploration is the natural differentiation that occurs based on the knowledge base of the students.

Sample Mathematics Lesson

Lesson Focus
This lesson focuses on the exploration of the elements of ratio and proportion. Students will use their understanding of fractional relationships to address the structure of the question, "Is the Statue of Liberty's nose too long?"

Objectives
- o   The student will demonstrate conceptual understanding of ratio and proportion.
- o   The student will provide a viable justification of the chosen solution.

CCSS-M Standards
- o   RPA.1
- o   7.RPA.2
- o   7.RPA.3

CCSS ELA Standards
- o   RST.6-8.1
- o   WHST.6-8.1.C
- o   WHST.6-8.2

Materials
- o   Actual dimensions of the Statue of Liberty
- o   Anatomy of human body
- o   Golden Ratio

Lesson Frame
The question, "Is the Statue of Liberty's nose too long?" will open the discussion for the lesson. Students will research the dimensions of the Statue of Liberty and the average length of human noses. Students will be encouraged to use a variety of strategies to determine the solution to the question posed. Each student will construct a journal entry demonstrating their solution and the rationale for the solution. Solutions will be shared and discussed as a class. The teacher will connect the strategies used by students to the concept of ratio and proportion. Students revisit their structures and ideas shared previously.

Extension Lesson
As students continue to develop their understandings of ratio and proportion, the extension lesson "Ratio and Proportion" will be introduced. With the teachers' guidance, students will have the opportunity to select DOK-leveled activities that are appropriate for their level of understanding.

LESSON 4.1
Computational Thinking

CCSS-M Mathematical Practices

» 1–8

Activities

The following sites have been divided based on the complexity of the mathematical practices involved in utilizing each site. Each of the sites listed is free for student use.

Set 1:

http://www.gethopscotch.com
http://www.alice.org
http://botlogic.us
http://www.kodable.com
http://www.madewithcode.com
http://www.codeavengers.com

Set 2:

https://scratch.mit.edu
http://www.jsdares.com
http://www.programmr.com
http://www.puzzleschool.com
http://www.code.org
http://www.codecademy.com

» Select a site within a group. Research the elements made available through the site. Make a chart sharing the advantages and disadvantages of the site. Give the site a rating based on your findings (DOK 1).
» Select one site from each of the sets. Compare the learning processes involved in each site. Prepare a proposal to convince your principal to allow students access to the coding activities (DOK 2).
» Select a Set 1 site and create a project utilizing 10–20 lines of code (DOK 2).
» Coding without a computer through unplugged activities offers learners another venue through which the material can be explored. Research

unplugged activities from this site (http://csunplugged.org/activities) and others. Assess the viability of learning coding through this format (DOK 3).

» Select a Set 2 site and create a project utilizing 10–20 lines of code (DOK 3).

» Replicate a coding project previously created using a Set 1 site. Use fewer lines of code than in the original (DOK 3).

» Replicate a coding project previously created using a Set 2 site. Use fewer lines of code than in the original (DOK 3).

» Select a coding site of your choice. Apply the coding concepts you have learned to design an original game and/or project. Your work should demonstrate your level of understanding and be accompanied by an explanation of your design process. Provide a critical analysis of your efforts (DOK 4).

LESSON 4.2
Algebraic Thinking

CCSS-M Standards

- » 8.EE.C.8
- » 8.EE.C.8.C
- » 8.F.A.2
- » 8.F.B.4

CCSS ELA Standards

- » RST.6-8.
- » RST.6-8.7
- » WHST.6-8.2

Activities

- » Demonstrate your quantitative reasoning skills. Write a letter to a friend explaining how many days are in a billion minutes without the use of calculations (DOK 1).
- » Using your understanding of linear equations, demonstrate how you would determined which is more cost efficient: a shower or a bath (DOK 2).
- » Functions play a role in algebraic thinking. Investigate a career that uses functions on a daily basis. What aspects of the job would be impacted without this mathematical understanding (DOK 2)?
- » Design and create a section of a roller coaster and evaluate the function. What other amusement park rides provide examples of nonlinear functions (DOK 2)?
- » Using point slope and your understanding of linear equations, select an animal that is currently hunted (e.g., deer, elk, javelins, or even quail). Based on Game and Fish population statistics, demonstrate how to calculate the size of the population in 10 years if natural predators and hunting were eliminated (DOK 3).
- » Linear equation systems allow one to compare data from multiple sources involving numerous factors. Select three major phone carriers. Identify a basic plan for each carrier that includes talk, text, and data. Evaluate when

one of the plans would be more cost effective and when they would cost the same. Based on your data, which carrier provides the best deal (DOK 3)?

» In the sequoia forest in northern California, would be more cost effective: to let a fire burn and extinguish itself or to put it out? Which choice would be better from an environmental perspective? Share your analysis using linear inequalities and systems. Prepare an rationale for your choice (DOK 4).

» Create a product designed to increase leisure time for the average student. Develop an equation to help determine your profit margin over a 3-year, 5-year, and 10-year period. Include the cost of materials, labor, and time. Does planned obsolescence factor into your formula? Prepare a presentation to share your business plan (DOK 4).

LESSON 4.3
Fractions

CCSS-M Standards

- » 6.RP.A.3
- » 6.RP.A.3.D

CCSS ELA Standards

- » RST.6-8.3
- » RST.6-8.7
- » WHST.6-8.2

Activities

- » Understanding precise language is critical in concept development. Define each of the vocabulary words for the fraction unit. Provide a sketch to deepen understanding (DOK 1).
- » Identify four ways the concepts in the fraction unit are represented in the real world. Demonstrate the connections discovered with these concepts (DOK 1).
- » Develop three anchor charts to represent key concepts learned in the unit. Your charts should provide a step-by-step guide to completion of the computational skills involved (DOK 2).
- » Using the whole numbers 1–9 at most one time each, create the largest fraction possible that is less than 1/2 and has a single digit in both the numerator and denominator. Justify your answer (DOK 2).
- » Develop an infographic to contrast and compare the relationships between fractions, percentages, and decimals. Summarize your findings (DOK 3).
- » Your school is planning an event. Due to the activities offered, not everyone will be seated at the same time. Three fifths of the people in a convention room are seated in 2/5 of the chairs and the remainder of the people decides to stand. If there are 27 empty chairs, how many people are standing? What strategies must be used to solve the Event Dilemma? Can it be solved in more that one way? Show as many solution strategies as you can (DOK 3).
- » Fractions play a key role in food preparation. Select two favorite recipes that require fractional portions. If you had only a 1/3 cup and a 1/2 teaspoon

to use, what modifications to the process of preparing the recipes would be needed. What impact does limiting the fraction options have on the preparation? Does it impact the final product? Provide a rationale for your decisions (DOK 3).

» Can we function from a time perspective without fractions? Develop a scenario for a world without fractional time components. Let your creativity flow as you design life without the increments that we have become accustomed to. Type your three- to four-page narrative. Offer a possible "Day in the Life of" scenario (DOK 4).

LESSON 4.4
Fermi Questions

CCSS Mathematical Practices

» 1, 2, 3, and 7

CCSS ELA Standards

» RST.6-8.2
» RST.6-8.7
» WHST.6-8.1
» WHST.6-8.6

Activities

» Research Enrico Fermi. "Fermi Questions" emphasize determining an answer on the correct order of magnitude instead of a specific number. Explain the goal of answering a Fermi Question (DOK 1).

» Respond to this Fermi Question, "How many pet dogs are in the United States?" Articulate your process (DOK 2).

» Fermi Questions require an understanding of the "order of magnitude." Explain this concept and represent it in a visual format. Provide two examples in support of your explanation (DOK 2).

» Respond to this Fermi Question, "How many Chinese restaurants exist in your town?" How does this question differ from the question asked in Question 2? Share your process and explanation (DOK 3).

» Fermi Questions have no right answers, only logical answers. Given that mathematics is about accuracy, justify the value of this type of mathematical exchange (DOK 3).

» Create a method or strategy for solving a Fermi Question. Outline your approach and have it critiqued by three classmates. Revise your strategy based on the input received. Design a presentation that shares your strategy (DOK 3).

» Design a set of four Fermi Questions across different mathematical domains to challenge your peers. Provide the structure needed to support solutions. Provide a logical solution for each problem (DOK 4).

» Defend or refute: "Estimation is part of our everyday experience. It is as valuable as the ability to determine an exact answer." Prepare a position paper in which you provide specific evidence in support of your stance (DOK 4).

LESSON 4.5
Multiple Intelligences Problem Solving

CCSS-M Mathematical Practice

» 1

CCSS ELA Standards

» WHST.6-8.1
» WHST.6-8.2
» WHST.6-8.9

Activities

Note. This extension lesson was creating using Gardner's Multiple Intelligences as the framework. The activities are designed to address the varied intelligences and are therefore not DOK leveled.

» Create and solve a story problem using only a pictorial representation (no words).
» Create a story problem that can be performed dramatically. Act out a story problem for the class.
» Compose a song that teaches the four steps to problem solving and perform it.
» Using a natural habitat of your choice, create a two-step story problem that includes the characteristics of that environment.
» Compare your work from a story problem with a partner and discuss the strategies you each used. Together come up with as many ways to solve the problem as possible.
» Solve a story problem and reflect in your journal about the strategies you used to get the answer.
» Write a multistep story problem that requires the use of a minimum of two operations.
» Debate which of the four steps of problem solving is the most important.

LESSON 4.6
Modeling With Mathematics

CCSS Mathematical Practice

» 4

CCSS ELA Standards

» RST.6-8.2
» RST.6-8.7
» WHST.6-8.1
» WHST.6-8.6

Activities

» Demonstrate how understanding patterns can enhance understanding of equations, and/or how the rules of probability operate in some aspect of life. Make a presentation demonstrating your findings (DOK 1).

» Investigate the math that is incorporated into activities that middle school students enjoy, such as skateboarding, soccer, basketball, football, or similar activities. Choose three of these activities and demonstrate the mathematics involved. Your demonstration can be in poster or multimedia format (DOK 2).

» Select five concepts that you or your peers have difficulty remembering. Create original mnemonics to help your peers remember these concepts. Concepts to consider include: order of operations, positive and negative integers, finding volume of geometric shapes, and other mathematical concepts. Present your mnemonics in an appropriate format (DOK 2).

» Create a presentation using real-world context to demonstrate the relationships between data, sample, probability, and statistics (DOK 3).

» Study the concept of Cartesian coordinates and find ways to explain their many facets that relate to real-world experience. Create a brochure to demonstrate these real-world connections (DOK 3).

» Create a comic strip to teach a favorite mathematical concept. Ask three peers to critique your work. Make modifications and then create a final strip (DOK 3).

» Surveys are a great way to gather information. Investigate how this type of data is used in the fields of marketing and advertising. Using Google forms, design a survey template that could be used to collect information on a product or topic of interest to teenagers. Deploy the survey and create a talking paper to present the results. Include the impact your data would have on the marketing and/or advertising of this product or topic (DOK 4).

» Design and conduct an experiment that demonstrates the difference between experimental and theoretical probability. Share your findings using data displays and reasoning (DOK 4).

LESSON 4.7
Ratios and Proportions

CCSS-M Standards

» RPA.1
» 7.RPA.2
» 7.RPA.3

CCSS ELA Standards

» RST.6-8.1
» WHST.6-8.1.C
» WHST.6-8.2

Activities

» There are several ways to represent a ratio. Provide each representation option and give examples that demonstrate when the representation would be used (DOK 1).

» Explain the difference between a ratio and a proportion. Give both examples and nonexamples to support your explanation (DOK 2).

» Cartographers use scales to represent distances on maps. Describe the connection between the use of scales and ratios. Discuss how changing the scale used on a map could alter the perception of distance (DOK 2).

» Architects, landscapers, and photographers all use ratios and proportions in their work. Select a career and show how an understanding of ratio and proportion is utilized. Give multiple examples to support your work (DOK 2).

» Examine the relationship between artistic perspective and mathematical ratio and proportion. Identify several artists that incorporate both areas into their work. Describe the effect the relationship generated (DOK 3).

» Do humans grow proportionally? Choose people of four ages ranging from infant to adult. Measure the same five body parts on each individual (e.g., head circumference, length of arm, etc.). Chart your findings and use your information to justify your answer (DOK 3).

» Read the poem "One Inch Tall" by Shel Silverstein. Write a similar poem in the same format. Your poem must use accurate proportional thinking to talk about the sizes of objects that you would use. Demonstrate at least three of the proportions you used to find the size of objects in your poem (DOK 4).

» Researchers believe that the numbers of fish in the Chesapeake Bay have decreased. Design an experiment using the concept of ratio and proportion to prove or disprove their theory (DOK 4).

LESSON 4.8
Geometry

CCSS-M Standard

» 6.G.A

CCSS ELA Standards

» RST.6-8.1
» RST.6-8.3
» RST.6-8.7

Activities

» Create a polygon book. Include illustrations, a description of attributes, identifiers of each angle, and the measurements of the angles of the polygons (DOK 1).

» Create a survey using Google forms to collect data regarding adults' knowledge of geometric terms. Survey a minimum of 25 adults. Prepare a presentation to present your results to the class. Your presentation should include graphic representations (DOK 2).

» Using your knowledge of geometric shapes, design your own unique 3D shape. Draw the shape including dimensions and estimate the volume (DOK 2).

» Using origami, create a design or use one that is familiar to you. Write step-by-step instructions utilizing only mathematical terminology: fractions, symmetry, faces, edges, triangle, rectangle, square, and rhombus. Record a video of your tutorial or create a presentation to present to the class (DOK 2).

» Construct a "place" (city, neighborhood, amusement park, etc.) using all unit geometric shapes in innovative ways. Label using math terminology (DOK 3).

» Tessellations are often used in modern art. Research four to five different modern artists to determine whether the artist used the tessellation technique. Demonstrate your findings and hypothesize why the artists may have used tessellations (DOK 3).

» Select a polygon. Design an advertisement that persuades the world that your polygon is more important than that of all other polygons (DOK 3).

» Design an invention that demonstrates your knowledge of geometric principles. Prepare a scaled drawing and a written explanation of its purpose and geometric attributes (DOK 4).

LESSON 4.9
Geometry Problem Solving

CCSS-M Standard

» 6.G.A

CCSS ELA Standards

» RST.6-8.3
» RST.6-8.7
» RST.6-8.9

Activities

» Your group has been assigned the task of bringing snacks for a trip. You decided to bring ice cream cones. The cones have ice cream on top wrapped in paper and come to a point, a perfectly shaped cone. Each cone with ice cream is 5 inches tall and has a diameter of 3 inches. You must figure out how many cones you should buy, if the rectangular prism cooler you are going to store them in is 12 inches by 22 inches by 11 inches. You will also put a bag of ice in the cooler. The bag of ice is shaped like a cylinder that is 10 inches in diameter and 18 inches tall. Represent your answer in graphically as well as with a detailed description (DOK 1).

» A fire simulation exercise is being conducted in a high-rise building. A 100-foot ladder is placed 35 feet away from a wall. The distance from the ground straight up to the top of the wall is 120 feet. The firefighters need to determine if their ladder is tall enough to reach the top floor. Create a diagram and determine whether the ladder reaches the top of the wall (DOK 2).

» A Design Central client is looking for a rectangular ottoman. They want one with the most storage space possible, but need a height between 14 inches and 16 inches. What are the options available in a rectangular design? What guidance would you provide as their salesperson? (DOK 2)

» You are designing a fish tank for production and need to know how much glass the tank will need as well as the volume the tank will hold. You do not want to spend more than $50 on glass, however you want to maximize the volume and the view the owner will have, while minimizing the cost and use of materials. Determine how you will do this. Present your findings providing graphic representation of the various designs (DOK 3).

» Create a design for a toy that demonstrates composite figures. Provide a scale drawing of the toy with all parts labeled. Give the surface area and volume of the toy (DOK 3).

» Peanuts, Peanuts, Peanuts is revamping their packaging. They need to determine which shape container will hold the most peanuts. They are open to any shape design. Develop a method to determine which shape has the greatest volume. Present your finding in a position paper to the company (DOK 3).

» An understanding of the concept of surface area and accuracy for computing it is needed in the business world. Identify three businesses that require the use of surface area to perform tasks. Interview two or more individuals from the business to gain an understanding of the significance that accuracy plays in the process. Compare the interviews and share your findings (DOK 4).

» Study the ways in which patterns on fabrics, wallpaper, tile, and other materials incorporate the principles of geometric concepts in the ways they are designed and used. Interview or research a designer to determine the impact of geometric design on the mood created. Incorporate the information obtained from your research with your own ideas. Design a visual to demonstrate how mood can be impacted by design options (DOK 4).

LESSON 4.10
Coordinate Plane

CCSS-M Standard

>> 6.G.A.3

CCSS ELA Standards

>> RST.6-8.4
>> RST.6-8.9

Activities

>> Create 8–10 nonstandard polygons. Calculate the areas of the nonstandard polygons using a coordinate plane (DOK 1).

>> Describe the following terms independently and in relation to each other: location and movement. Use common language and geometric vocabulary (DOK 1).

>> Coordinate planes are used in computer graphics, animation, and other creative endeavors. Select one endeavor. Design a graphic organizer to share the relationship between the elements of the coordinate plane and the endeavor chosen (DOK 2).

>> Using coordinate planes, create a drawing, maze, or tessellation pattern, and prepare the directions for a user to make that product happen by following your exact directions. Compare both products and explain any discrepancies (DOK 2).

>> Coordinate planes can be used to specify locations and/or describe pathways to the locations. Make and demonstrate the use of coordinate systems for this purpose. Create a tutorial explaining your work (DOK 2).

>> Compare and contrast the polar coordinate system and the linear coordinate system regarding their construction and uses. Provide real-world examples of the two systems in a display format (DOK 3).

>> Investigate how coordinate planes are used in city planning, military maneuvers, meteorology, and/or another field. Select two fields of study, and contrast and compare the use of coordinate planes within the fields. Create a visual graphic representation to share your results (DOK 3).

» Identify the key concepts needed to understand coordinate planes. Design a presentation to connect these concepts to how coordinate grids/planes are used in solving real-world problems in different fields, such as crime scene investigations, resource management, or space exploration. Include precise vocabulary and examples in support of your analysis (DOK 4).

LESSON 4.11
Polygons and Angles

CCSS-M Standards

- » 6.G.A.1
- » 7.G.B.5
- » HSG.SRT.C.6

CCSS ELA Standards

- » RST.6-8.3
- » RST.6-8.7
- » WHST.6-8.2

Activities

- » Design a polygon matrix. Include illustrations, description of attributes, identifiers of each angle, and the measurements of the angles contained within the polygons (DOK 1).
- » Using regular or irregular polygons, draw and cut out a shape to tessellate. Trace and arrange the polygons to form a tessellation pattern. Measure all of the interior angles. Then determine the measurements of each exterior angle (DOK 1).
- » Find the sum of the interior angles in any polygon by dividing it up into triangles with lines connecting the vertices. Determine the sum of all the interior angles of the polygon and create a table that examines the relationship between them and the sum of all the angles in each triangle. Repeat the same analysis for the following shapes: (a) quadrilateral, (b) pentagon, (c) heptagon, (d) octagon, (e) nonagon, (f) dodecagon, and (g) compound shapes. Once you have completed the table, determine the formula for the sum of the interior angles of a polygon with n sides (DOK 2).
- » Create a digital scavenger hunt for angles and triangles in the real world, photograph them, and identify them. Identify and measure the angles depicted in the photographs. Create a digital presentation categorizing the work by topic: acute, right, obtuse, complementary, supplementary, vertical, and adjacent angles (DOK 2).

» Create step-by-step instructions on how to draw a particular figure using only a protractor. You must include the angles and the exact measurement of the lines in mm and cm. Make sure to use proper terminology in your instructions and precise language (DOK 3).

» Construct a map using angles, lines, and line segments. Your task is to design a map that includes several different kinds of lines, angles, and triangles. Include the following: streets that are parallel; streets that are perpendicular; streets that intersect another to form an obtuse angle; streets that intersect another to form an acute angle; streets that intersect another to form a right angle; streets that intersect another to form an adjacent angles; streets that intersect another to form an complementary angles; streets that intersect another to form supplementary angles; streets that include line segments; and streets that are lines. Include a compass rose in your map. Once your map is completed, write out directions from one place to another. Using appropriate academic terminology (DOK 3).

» Two friends were arguing about the best seat in the movie theatre. One of them had heard that it is best to sit so that the angle formed by the line of sight between the left and right sides of the screen is 30 degrees. Arturo believes there is only one seat in the theatre that meets these criteria. Angelica argues there is more than one place where the viewing angle is also 30 degrees. Decide who is correct and prove it (DOK 3).

» Create geodesic domes using origami. Using Euler's formula, count vertices, edges, and faces, and then solve a system of linear equations. Place this information in a table. Analyze the data and determine the relationships between the number of pentagon faces, hexagon faces, edges, and vertices (DOK 4).

LESSON 4.12
Geometric Thinking in Sports

CCSS-M Standard

» 6.G.A

CCSS ELA Standards

» RST.6-8.1
» RST.6-8.3
» RST.6-8.7

Activities

» Find examples of geometric shapes that exist in sports. Locate examples of these shapes and identify them based on their angles (DOK 1).

» Research a sports-related career that uses geometry. Include where you can receive an education that might lead to this profession (DOK 1).

» Create a how-to book for finding missing angle measures that is sports-themed. Share with a student who is struggling in this area and ask for a critique of your work (DOK 2).

» Pick a favorite beverage or food item served at a sporting event and design a new container for it. You must include the specific dimensions of the container and make sure that it holds just as much in volume as the original. Describe why your new container is better than the previous model (DOK 3).

» Research three different Major League Baseball stadiums. Compare and contrast their outfield dimensions. Take into consideration the back wall height and determine which stadium you believe would be the easiest in which to hit a home run. Gather home run statistics for each field to support or refute your choice (DOK 3).

» Aluminum baseball bats are not allowed in Major League Baseball, however, they are used in college baseball. Research the average trajectory of pitches hit using both types of bats. Which is easier to hit a home run with? Hypothesize why this could be the case (DOK 3).

» Using http://www.surfline.com and the swell ruler, measure how long it takes a storm's swells to reach San Diego beaches if the storm originates in the Antarctic. Identify factors impacting the height of the swells. At what angle will the swells arrive at the San Diego beaches? Contract and compare this to the swells' arrival in Hawaii (DOK 4).

» Design a new hole for a local golf course. Research the dimensions of the current hole using Google Earth and propose a new more challenging hole. Be sure to include all of the new dimensions for the new hole. Provide a rationale for changing to your more challenging format (DOK 4).

LESSON 4.13
Math Studies

CCSS Mathematical Practices

» 1–8

CCSS ELA Standards

» RST.6-8.3
» RST.6-8.7
» WHST.6-8.2

Activities

» Research the biography of a famous mathematician and write about his or her experience with education in his or her childhood. Create a timeline (DOK 1).

» Develop a set of five to eight word problems involving a current math topic that you are learning. Create step-by-step solutions to these word problems (DOK 2).

» Demonstrate alternate ways and strategies to solve word problems for the chapter you are currently working on (DOK 2).

» Investigate the real-world applications related to the current math topic you are learning. Design a graphic to represent the connections found (DOK 2).

» Word problems often present a challenge to students. Research different strategies for attacking word problems. Identify their similarities and differences. Summarize your findings and select the strategy you feel is the most successful. Provide a rationale with examples for your selection (DOK 3).

» Learning styles and strengths can impact a learner's ability to understand content fully. Holistic learners are often frustrated by a part-to-part approach. Analyze and identify different ways to explain the current math topic to your classmates (DOK 3).

» Investigate and draw conclusions about how math impacts the world today. Hypothesize the percentage of the careers today requiring mathematical proficiency? Has the number increased or decreased over the last 10 years? Support your stand (DOK 4).

» How has the development of algebra directly impacted your life or the life of your family? Create a presentation sharing "algebra" of your life (DOK 4).

LESSON 4.14
Famous Mathematicians

CCSS ELA Standards

- » RST.6-8.5
- » WHST 6-8.2
- » WHST.6-8.2.B
- » WHST.6-8.2.A

Activities

Select a mathematician from the list:

- » Blaise Pascal
- » Isaac Barrow
- » Sir Isaac Newton
- » Felix Christian Klein
- » Leonardo Pisano Bigollo (Fibonacci)
- » Christopher Clavius
- » Eratosthenes of Cyrene
- » Edmond Halley
- » Archimedes
- » Galileo Galilei
- » Maria Agnesi
- » Robert Boyle
- » Augustus De Morgan
- » Zeno of Elea
- » Johannes Kepler
- » Bertrand Russell
- » Albert Einstein
- » Charles Lutwidge Dodgson
- » Euclid of Alexandria
- » Dame Mary Lucy Cartwright
- » David Hilbert
- » Plato
- » Aristotle
- » Nicholas Copernicus
- » Bernhard Riemann
- » Georg Ferdinand Cantor
- » Hippocrates of Chios
- » Louis Braille

- » Create a timeline for your chosen mathematician. Provide details of his or her personal life as well as his or her mathematical contributions (DOK 1).
- » Contrast and compare the lives of two mathematicians from different eras. Create a Venn diagram. How did the time period in which they lived impact their work (DOK 2)?
- » In 1821, Frenchman Louis Braille developed a method that is used to help blind people read and write. This system was based on a more complicated process of communication that was formed by Charles Barbier. Braille decided to simplify the code by using a six-dot cell because the human finger

needed to cover the entire symbol without moving so that it could progress quickly from one symbol to the next. Using the six-dot Braille cell, how many different combinations are possible? An extension has been added to the Braille code that contains eight dots with the two additional ones added to the bottom. How does this change the number of possible different combinations? Justify your answer by providing a detailed explanation. What are the implications of adding additional dots to the Braille system (DOK 3)?

» Evaluate the character traits that are found among the great mathematicians. Create a character analysis based on your findings. What qualities do these individuals share? Make a prioritized list of the qualities identified through your character analysis. Explain your method of prioritization (DOK 3).

» In *Time* magazine's The Most Influential People of the 20th Century, the names of 100 influential people are organized into groups and ranked in order of their importance. Who do you view as the top five mathematical leaders? Create your own magazine with articles on your selections. Include a photo of the individual as well as relevant data written in expository form in each article (DOK 3).

» What would our current world be like if your selected mathematician had not made his or her discoveries? Provide a graphic to show the implications that the loss of this knowledge would have on generations to follow (DOK 3).

» Write an autobiography for one of the identified mathematicians. Include information that the individual would have wanted to share that may or may not have related to his or her mathematical life (DOK 3).

» One can learn a great deal about a person from his or her desk. If you had the opportunity to look through the desk of your favorite mathematician, what treasures would you find? Identify 10 items from the desk and justify their significance to the mathematical life of the individual. Sometimes it isn't only what we find that is of importance, but what we don't find. Hypothetically if there was an item missing from the desk that you expected to find, what would that item be? Why do you believe this item might be missing? What does the missing item add to your understanding of the individual (DOK 4)?

LESSON 4.15
Science, Technology, Engineering, and Math (STEM)

NGSS Standard

» MS-PS1-3

CCSS ELA Standards

» RST.6-8.9
» WHST.6-8.1
» WHST.6-8.7
» WHST.6-8.8

Activities

» Research the history of rockets. Starting with Archytas in 400 B.C., create a pictorial timeline. Be sure to include dates, events, illustrations, and descriptions (DOK 1).

» The Space Launch System (SLS) has five primary objectives. Research each objective and the role it plays in the overall goals of the space program (DOK 1).

» Compare and contrast the advantages and disadvantage of liquid and solid propellant rockets. Prepare a presentation to share your findings (DOK 2).

» Identify and summarize Newton's laws of motion. Select one of the laws and demonstrate its relationship to the science of rocketry (DOK 2).

» Research the classic aeoliphile engine invented by Hero of Alexandria. Using soda pop cans, carpenter nails, string, and water create an aeoliphile engine or a digital depiction of one. Identify the forces that keep the cans in motion (DOK 3).

» Space art supports the exploration of space. Early space art was created using traditional materials and techniques. Many space artists still portray their dreams this way, but computer graphics has also found a place in space art. Research the use of technology, particularly computer graphics, on space art. Using technology, demonstrate how it has impacted this art form (DOK 3).

» Rocket stability is an issue for rocket scientists. What aspects of design make a rocket stable? Using paper rockets to test your hypotheses. Report your results (DOK 4).

» Use your understanding of Newton's laws of motion. Design a rocket using air or water as a propellant. Conduct 4–5 test flights altering flight and stability variables with each launch. Critique and modify your design based on your findings (DOK 4).

5

Science Extension Lessons

Introduction

Science is a content-driven discipline that is systematic and seeks to build and organize knowledge in such a way that it can be tested and replicated. Science attempts to explain the unexplainable phenomena of our world; it is the unending search for truth. The scientific method is one of discipline, laws, and observable behaviors. Science demands that measurements be accurate and that observations be clearly made without bias.

Preassessment

Preassessment in the sciences may look differently than in other content areas. Given the skill base needed, as well as the degree of process understanding that students must demonstrate, teachers often elect to preassess primarily for basic vocabulary and knowledge. When preassessment is used in this manner, extension lessons enrich and deepen student understandings rather than accelerate or compact curriculum. Using benchmark assessments or unit tests to determine what students know allows the teacher to facilitate a deeper conceptual understanding through the DOK activities selected.

Connections to Standards

With the implementation of the CCSS for ELA (NGA & CCSSO, 2010a) teachers must incorporate literacy skills within the detail-oriented elements of their discipline. Embedding ELA into the curriculum today means more than writing a lab report or researching and reporting on a scientist. Literacy skills must now be embedded into all aspects of the science curriculum. As an example, this can be seen in the need to read and understand vocabulary-dense text and when developing analytical skills related to the scientific method. The Next Generation Science Standards (NGSS) challenge students to participate in a three-dimensional learning experience as the standards are explored. They focus students on the practices, the crosscutting concepts, as well as the disciplinary core structures for the demonstration of proficiencies.

Connections to DOK Levels

The extension lessons in this chapter provide students with opportunities to practice and embed literacy and critical thinking skills into science content at both instructional and challenge levels. By selecting the appropriate DOK level, the teacher and students can ensure the appropriate challenge level is being addressed, while also closely adhering to the science standards.

All four DOK levels can provide students with opportunities for the type of analysis required for the study of scientific information. Within DOK Level 1, recall of information requires the student to identify, recognize, measure, and calculate using basic procedures and simple science processes. At this level, word problems are simple and can be directly translated and solved by a formula. Problems found in Level 1 do not require the student to "figure it out;" in these problems, the answer is either known or could be identified in text. For example, a Level 1 activity would require a student to identify a scientific property or perform a routine task, such as measuring the mass of an object.

Sample Lesson

In the sample science lesson included in this chapter, a Level 1 activity requires students to select a disease and research its impact on human body. Students create a brochure or some form of presentation documenting the research. Information contained would include symptoms, treatments, and a list of patient resources. This level of complexity requires students to locate and recall material read.

An increase in complexity within each lesson is found as students move from DOK Level 1 to Level 2. In Level 2, students make a determination of how to approach the problem. The students must determine relevance of data by making observations and then drawing conclusions based on their observation. This is very similar to what we see in Level 2 in the content area of mathematics. At this level, students are required to describe examples, as well as nonexamples, of a scientific concept. Students would collect, organize, and interpret data and then present the information in graphic as well as written format.

As students progress and need more complex learning activities, they can explore extension activities in DOK Levels 3 and 4. The level of abstract reasoning required in Level 3 activities differentiates it from those found in Levels 1 and 2. Experimental designs in Level 3 typically involve more than one dependent variable. Within the context of science, Level 3 activities include actions such as drawing conclusions from observations, citing evidence and developing a logical argument for concepts, explaining phenomena in terms of concepts, and using concepts to solve nonroutine problems. At this level, justification of one's reasoning is a key outcome. Students working on Level 3 extension activities must be able to articulate their understandings using precise and accurate language. In some science lessons, the ability to provide a clear and accurate justification is what separates the Level 3 extensions from those in Level 2.

Level 4 extension lesson activities extend the level of cognitive thought as well as the degree of complexity required for the student to demonstrate understanding. A Level 4 activity might require a student to develop generalizations based on results obtained from two separate or differing accounts and then synthesize and apply these generalizations to a new problem or existing situation. The increase in rigor in science at this level is often found in complex reasoning, experimental design, and students' planning. Level 4 activities may also contain a degree of novelty and intrigue for students and requires that they make deductions about the relationships between several controlled variables.

By providing students with activities from all four DOK levels, teachers can support the varied learning needs within the regular classroom, as well as the advanced needs of students in an honors or Advanced Placement science class. The example lesson on the human body shows students moving from whole-group instruction to small-group work. You will see students working on learning activities that are structured for the students' varying challenge levels.

Sample Science Lesson

Utilizing patterns and relationships as a means of examining content allows high-ability learners to extend their thinking beyond the confines of the curriculum. In this lesson, students will use the content knowledge acquired to build a justification of need for an identified body organ. Students use persuasive writing techniques along with their understandings of the interrelated workings of the organs of the body to establish their justification. As students work through the research component of this lesson, they are provided with the extension lesson "Human Body." The teacher guides students in exploring specific depth and complexity levels within the extension lesson. The teacher supports the students as they select an appropriate DOK level activity.

Lesson Focus

To establish the role of body organs and their interrelationships through supporting evidence.

Objectives

- o The student will research a selected body organ and identify its role within the body system.
- o The student will determine the significance of the performance of the chosen organ in relation to the body's survival.
- o The student will prepare a persuasive letter outlining the performance of the organ and its overall significance within the body.

NGSS Standards

- o MS-LS1-3
- o MS-LS1-2

Materials

- o Research materials and/or Internet access
- o Set of organ cards

Lesson Frame

Students will complete a pretest demonstrating their level of knowledge with regard to basic organ functions. Based on the results of the pretest, students are provided with tiered research materials to structure and support the research process.

Students draw an organ card from the box. They have 2 days to research the role that the organ plays in the human body. As part of their research, the student create a multimedia presentation explaining the functions of the organ and its significance for the body's function.

On Day 3, students are informed of the following scenario:

The Human Body Corporation wishes to inform you that due to rising costs, your body organ has been placed on the elimination list. You need to provide a letter to the corporation justifying removing your organ from the elimination list.

On Day 4, students are grouped into teams of four or five. Within the team, they must decide which of the team's organs will be eliminated and make a presentation to the Human Body Corporation explaining their selection and the impact it will have upon the body as a whole. Presentations will be shared with the class.

Closure: Reflect on the process of determining a selection.

Extension Lesson

As students begin conducting their research and then write their persuasive letter, the teacher works individually to guide students to the DOK level of extension appropriate to meet their challenge needs. The teacher provides students time to work on their extension lesson selection each day as the lesson progresses. In this manner, students are provided with the additional challenge needed and given an opportunity to extend their thinking.

LESSON 5.1
Cells and Microorganisms

NGSS Standards

- » MS-LS1-1
- » MS-LS1-2
- » MS-LS1-3

CCSS ELA Standards

- » RST.6-8.3
- » WHST.6-8.1

Activities

- » Create an illustrated timeline showing/describing the development of the microscope to present time. Include visual examples of the cellular views that microscopes have provided throughout the time frame (DOK 1).
- » Create a physical or digital 3D model of a eukaryote cell, a prokaryote cell, and a virus. Color code, label, and include a key for the models (DOK 1).
- » Choose an exotic location that you would be interested in visiting on vacation. Research infectious diseases common to that area. Create a message or posting that will prepare tourists for diseases that they may encounter (bacterial, viral, and protista). Include information about how they can recognize and avoid these diseases and about available treatment (DOK 2).
- » Pretend you are a reporter who can converse with a cellular organelle. Interview a cellular organelle and write an article for the school newspaper about the organelle (DOK 2).
- » You are a healthcare worker speaking to Congress to request funding for AIDS treatment. Write a persuasive speech stating why you should receive funding. Include data that supports your position. Explain why your cause should be funded above other causes (DOK 3).
- » Create a recipe booklet. Each recipe must use bacteria, fungus, or protists as an important ingredient (at least one of each). Explain how the microorganism is important to each recipe. Provide an illustration of each prepared dish (DOK 3).

» Create an analogy comparing the organelles of a eukaryotic cell to the parts of a city (e.g., lysosome = recycling center). Include a table describing the organelles' real function and their functions in your analogy (DOK 3).

» Design and carry out an experiment to determine which nontoxic household items prevent mold growth on bread. Explain how a nontoxic item can prevent the growth of a toxic one (DOK 4).

LESSON 5.2
Cell Structure

NGSS Standards

- » MS-LS1-1
- » MS-LS1-2
- » MS-LS1-3

CCSS ELA Standards

- » RST.6-8.1
- » RST.6-8.9
- » WHST.6-8.1
- » WHST.6-8.2
- » WHST.6-8.8

Activities

- » Study the cellular anomalies that cause birth defects. Explain how modern technology is addressing the problems created by a defect in an unborn child. Select one anomaly and report on the information (DOK 1).
- » Research famous incidents of multiple births. Demonstrate how unusual cell division leads to such occurrences. Examine the relationship of the chemistry of fertility drugs to the events of multiple births (DOK 2).
- » Study a field related to cell structure, such as cytology, histology, biochemistry, etc. Investigate careers related to that field during current times. Document the ways in which the jobs within one of those careers have changed over the past decade (DOK 2).
- » Study the thalidomide event of the 1950s. Find other examples of how a drug designed for benefit created harm. Investigate the use of thalidomide today for symptoms other than the ones for which it was originally intended. Describe methods or procedures scientists have used to prevent a similar event from happening since that event (DOK 3).
- » Research a disease that comes from out-of-control cell division. Learn about emerging treatments that appear efficacious. Investigate experimental and unique approaches to eliminating that disease (DOK 3).

» In rare instances, multiple births produce conjoined children. Research several such cases. Investigate the role current methods and technologies play in supporting the lives of these children (DOK 4).

» Learn about the issues surrounding cloning and explain the process. Consider the issue from several points of view (i.e., scientists, doctors, religious leaders and farmers) and examine the ethical considerations that each of these groups might express. Include your personal views on this topic if you feel comfortable doing so. Create a position paper or presentation to share your findings (DOK 4).

» Hirano bodies are important but poorly understood cell structures. Scientists hope they will eventually provide critical information regarding the prevention and/or treatment of mysterious diseases such as Alzheimer's, Lou Gehrig's disease, and others. Learn what you can about this topic and decide if you feel it offers true hope to people who suffer from these and similar diseases. Support your findings in a pro/con format (DOK 4).

LESSON 5.3
Cells

NGSS Standards

- » MS-LS1-1
- » MS-LS1-2
- » MS-LS1-3

CCSS ELA Standards

- » RST.6-8.3
- » RST.6-8.7
- » WHST.6-8.1
- » WHST.6-8.4

Activities

- » Choose an organ of the human body and describe how it functions at the cellular, tissue, organ, and organ system level in humans (DOK 1).
- » Investigate other things, besides plant, animal, or human cells, that use the word "cell" to describe them. Collect and display illustrations representing how this word applies in different categories (DOK 1).
- » Research and report on the life and work of a scientist who has worked in an area of cell research (DOK 2).
- » Research why cells are referred to as the "building blocks of life." Describe how they function in multicellular organisms. Construct a framework to explain your findings (DOK 2).
- » Go online or use an electronic microscope to examine at least three types of plant cells. Take digital pictures and label their parts. In your presentation, compare and contrast the cells you study (DOK 2).
- » Investigate careers that are connected in some way to the study of cells. Select and examine one that interests you. Create a job application form and/or interview questions that you believe would help interviewers find the right person for the job (DOK 3).
- » Design a model city based on the functionality of cell organelles. Create a blueprint of the city. Identify each component and its connection to the function of the organelle within the cell structure (DOK 3).
- » Design a lab experience that creates a learning experience for students to observe the differences between plant and animal cells (DOK 4).

LESSON 5.4
Human Body

NGSS Standards

- » MS-LS1-3
- » MS-LS3-1

CCSS ELA Standards

- » RST.6-8.1
- » RST.6-8.5
- » WHST.6-8.1
- » WHST.6-8

Activities

- » Create an educational message for your classmates that explains the function of a body system. Include domain specific terminology in describing the body system (DOK 1).
- » Research a disease. Write an informational campaign that describes the disease and how it affects the human body. Include the symptoms of the disease and the new technologies and advancements in health care that address the disease. Provide a list of resources for patients to get more information on the disease (DOK 2).
- » Identify a disorder of a body system that interests you. Create a list of interview questions one would ask a professional about the disorder. Interview a healthcare professional to glean information. Create an announcement based on the interview to teach the public about the disorder (DOK 2).
- » Create a game that will teach your classmates about a particular body system. Include facts about the body system, its organs, their functions, and how they work together. Provide a set of directions with your game (DOK 2).
- » Research the effects of a high fat diet on the human body. Study its effects on the heart and circulatory system, and develop a logical argument of how it could affect the other systems of the body (DOK 3).
- » Use research to explain the effect of temperature on muscle action. Create a video, guide, or tutorial that teaches proper warm-up exercises that can

reduce muscle strain and tearing. Cite research as evidence behind your informational video (DOK 3).

» Create a detailed model of one of the systems of the human body. Label each organ of the body system and write a report or create a presentation describing how the organs work together for the functioning of the body system and factors that can lead to the problem (DOK 3).

» Create a digital model that represents the connection between the skeletal and muscle systems and how they function for movement. Record a demonstration video of your model and include an explanation of the musculoskeletal system. Use the context of a sports figure to support your explanation of the connection (DOK 4).

LESSON 5.5
Life Sciences

NGSS Standard

» MS-LS1-2

CCSS ELA Standards

» RST.6-8.1
» RST.6-8.8
» WHST.6-8.1
» WHST.6-8.9

Activities

» Create a diagram of a human cell and label all of its parts. Include a written description of the function of each part of a cell. Write a detailed description of how each part works together for cellular function (DOK 1).

» Examine the existence of "super viruses" that appear to resist present medical interventions. Research how agencies, such as the Center for Disease Control, work to prevent pandemic outbreaks of disease. Create an informational presentation of your findings (DOK 2).

» Study the research on DNA. Report on its impact on advancements in medicine, agriculture, criminal investigations, and other topics. Chart your findings (DOK 2).

» Compare the usual effects of mitosis in the human body to what happens when mitosis goes out of control through ultra rapid, uncontrolled divisions. Describe the divisions, then investigate and report on emerging therapies to prevent this harmful situation (DOK 3).

» Study two environmental issues that have significant impacts on human health and well-being in the beginning of this century. Provide examples of efforts being made to address these issues (DOK 3).

» Stem cell research has advanced significantly in recent years. Examine and report on the controversies surrounding this research, including the possibilities of human cloning. Take a position on this controversy and develop a logical argument supporting your position about how stem cells could/should be utilized (DOK 3).

» Research ways in which the breakdown of one part of a cell can affect the workings of the cell's other parts. In your discussion, report on ways damaged cell parts can be repaired. Create a demonstration that teaches your audience about this interaction (DOK 3).

» The field of cancer treatment is continually exploring new ways to fight the disease. Identify new or emerging treatments and based on your research, hypothesize as to which ones have the most promise for reducing deaths from cancer. Describe ways for patients to learn about new treatment options (DOK 4).

LESSON 5.6
Acids and Bases

NGSS Standard

» MS-PS1-2

CCSS ELA Standards

» RST.6-8.3
» RST.6-8.9
» WHST.6-8.1
» WHST.6-8.9

Activities

» Using a hydrangea plant, calculate the amount of an acid or base necessary to change the flower's color from blue to pink. Provide a step-by-step analysis of your calculations (DOK 1).

» Answer the following questions and depict your responses in a format of your choosing (DOK 1). Keep in mind that (a) the pH indicator will be the right one to balance the amount of acid and base, (b) not all titrations are acid, and (c) for base titrations, there is an indicator that will tell when molar amounts are matched.

 ◆ 23.45 mL of 0.275 M sodium hydroxide was used to titrate against 12 mL of acetic acid. What was the concentration in M of acetic acid?

 ◆ 17.05 mL of 0.247 M barium hydroxide was used to titrate against 10 mL of nitric acid. What was the concentration in M of nitric acid?

 ◆ 35.79 mL of 0.275 M sodium hydroxide was used to titrate against 15 mL of sulfuric acid. What was the concentration in M of sulfuric acid?

 ◆ 24.92 mL of 0.00199 M silver nitrate was used to titrate against 5 mL of sodium chloride solution. What was the concentration of NaCl?

» Describe and demonstrate the safety precautions required both inside and outside a lab when handling acids and bases. Report on the effects of possible consequences when appropriate precautions are not taken (DOK 2).

» Analyze 10–15 different acids and bases and determine their H_3O or OH (levels) by measuring pH first. Rate them from weak to strong (DOK 2).

» Create a game in which students must show mastery of the properties of acids and bases (DOK 2).

» Cleaning agents are developed using a variety of chemicals. Does a base make a good cleaning agent? Determine how the chemistry changes between regular cleaning agents and those that claim benefits from oxygen. Develop and present an argument supporting the use of a cleaning agent with or without oxygen (DOK 3).

» Search your home to find and identify several acids and bases at work in the kitchen, bathroom, garage, and other locations. Create a SMART card, a card that offers a detailed explanation of how to avoid problems when working with these substances (DOK 3).

» Using a Microscale technique (or similar technology), design and demonstrate a neutralization chemical reaction between an acid and a base. Explain your process in detail (DOK 4).

LESSON 5.7
Periodic Table

NGSS Standard

» MS-PS1-1

CCSS ELA Standards

» RST.6-8.1
» RST.6-8.7
» RST.6-8.9
» WHST.6-8.1
» WHST.6-8.4
» WHST.6-8.9

Activities

» Investigate how string physics affects or is affected by the Periodic Table. Create a concept map of your findings (DOK 1).
» Choose an element from the Periodic Table to research and visually represent your data (DOK 1). Describe:
  ♦ its atomic number;
  ♦ its atomic mass, arrangement, and groups;
  ♦ its stability;
  ♦ the elements it reacts with; and
  ♦ where the element is found.

» Identify and study the pioneering scientists who developed the Periodic Table. Describe their efforts in designing this tabular arrangement of the chemical elements (DOK 2).
» Write an informational paper and create a presentation describing the usefulness of the Periodic Table from its inception to the present day (DOK 2).
» Compare and contrast the differences that hydrogen has to other elements in Group 1 of the Periodic Table. Present your information according: properties, covalent bonds, and stability. Do the same with one element of another group. Then identify and discuss pertinent differences between the two (DOK 3).

» Prioritize the elements most used in our daily life and construct a different Periodic Table for those elements. Justify your selections (DOK 3).

» Combine two elements to create a new, third element. Create a visual representation of the new element (DOK 3). Include a description of the new element's:

- covalent bonds,
- stability, and
- suggested precautions.

» Create a (digital or physical) 3D representation of several atoms and explain their inner and outer structures. Describe and explain how these differences affect the elements when combined with other elements. Identify how a simple change in the inner or outer structure would impact the atom's ability to combine to form a desired element (DOK 4).

LESSON 5.8
Stoichiometry

NGSS Standard

» MS-PS1-5

CCSS ELA Standards

» RST.6-8.1
» RST.6-8.9
» WHST.6-8.
» WHST.6-8.2

Activities

» Research the process by which a medication, food item, fertilizer, or other substance is synthesized. Produce a step-by-step explanation of the process (DOK 1).

» Study and describe ways that stoichiometry is used to improve the quality of everyday life (DOK 1).

» Using current events or an article from the Internet, describe how stoichiometry might be used to determine the amount of pollutants that could be produced in your state or region in one month. Create a chart to share your findings (DOK 2).

» Modify a cooking recipe using stoichiometry to obtain the requested yield. Contrast and compare the two recipes (DOK 2).

» Jeremiah Richter first laid down the principles of stoichiometry. Examine his journey and identify stumbling blocks that led to the development of this field of learning. Create a timeline of his life and achievements (DOK 2).

» Design an original concept map that examines the significance of stoichiometry to the scientific world. Cite references in support of your explanations (DOK 3).

» Identify an artistic or other venue in which a concept similar to stoichiometry is found. Describe and evaluate the relationships between the two venues. Create a presentation to share your findings (DOK 3).

» Design and conduct an investigation to illustrate the following concepts (DOK 4):

- balancing equations,
- stoichiometry/mole ratios,
- limiting reactants, and
- theoretical yields, actual yields, and percentage yields.

LESSON 5.9
Heat

NGSS Standards

» MS-PS3-3

CCSS ELA Standards

» RST.6-8.1
» RST.6-8.4
» RST.6-8.9
» WHST.6-8.2

Activities

» Describe the process involved in heating a home (DOK 1).

» Create a vocabulary web model demonstrating your understanding of the scientific concept of heat (DOK 1).

» Make a concept map showing how heat affects matter during a change of state and during a chemical change (DOK 2).

» Use the concept of specific heat capacity to explain why coastal cities have milder temperatures year-round than inland cities. Create a concept map or graphic organizer to demonstrate your understanding (DOK 2).

» Research the life of two of the following: Anders Celsius, Daniel Gabriel Fahrenheit, William Rankine, and William Thomson (Lord Kelvin). Create a project in which you describe the relationship between their work and assess the significance of their combined efforts (DOK 3).

» Study the controversy regarding Freon's effect on the environment. Research the alternatives to Freon. Compare and contrast it to other alternatives. Present your findings (DOK 3).

» Learn how insulating materials are rated. What are the R-values based on and what R-values are recommended for your area? Create a demonstration to teach the general public about this topic (DOK 3).

» Research and discuss what occurs when energy has been transferred by heat. Create an experiment that demonstrates this principle. Explain your findings in a science log that includes primary source information (DOK 4).

LESSON 5.10
Force and Motion

NGSS Standards

- » MS-PS2-1
- » MS-PS2-2
- » MS-PS2-4
- » MS-PS2-5

CCSS ELA Standards

- » RST.6-8.3
- » WHST.6-8.1
- » WHST.6-8.8
- » WHST.6-8.9

Activities

- » Design a flipbook that demonstrates Newton's Laws. Include examples from the laws of motion that are exemplified in space travel (DOK 1).
- » Describe and illustrate how an object's size and its distance from other objects affect gravity (DOK 1).
- » Study movies and TV shows in which movement defies the laws of force and motion. Use scientific terminology to explain why such movement would not be possible (DOK 2).
- » Create a presentation explaining the phenomena of gravitational forces on an object in terms of concepts related to the sun and moon's relative influence on gravity (DOK 2).
- » Create a presentation that demonstrates how various forces affect motion. Forces might include: action, reaction, equilibrium conditions, free-falling objects, etc. Explain this phenomenon using domain specific terminology and evidence (DOK 3).
- » Research experiments that demonstrate one of Newton's Laws. Then create and perform one of your own. Include examples from the laws of motion that are exemplified in space travel (DOK 3).

» Research and examine experiments that demonstrate how energy interacts with matter to conserve mass and energy. Consider and describe possible future uses and outcomes for each interaction (DOK 4).

» Design and perform an experiment that explains how interactions of energy and matter affect changes of state. Discuss real-world examples of how these interactions may or may not have profound or lasting impacts on an area. Predict the implications of your findings to future research (DOK 4).

LESSON 5.11
Light and Sound

NGSS Standard

» MS-PS4-2

CCSS ELA Standards

» RST.6-8.1
» RST.6-8.7
» RST.6-8.9
» WHST.6-8.1
» WHST.6-8.4

Activities

» Describe how lasers are used in the treatment of the human body. Explain why the use of optical fibers to pipe energy deep inside the body has replaced many conventional surgical procedures (DOK 1).

» Create a presentation in which you describe how light and sound waves travel (DOK 1).

» Identify and present on particle-wave theories of light. Include information on several scientists involved in this work to describe the similarities and differences in their approach to their work in this field (DOK 2).

» Research how lasers are used in other fields of science and work. Predict how their use will impact their fields and impact life for humans in future generations. Create a possible timeline of future uses (DOK 3).

» Create an interactive activity for your classmates that will allow them to determine how several types of instruments vibrate, how pitch is created, and how frequency affects sound (DOK 3).

» Design an experiment that determines how color affects the temperature of an object when light is shone upon the object. Relate your findings to the color of animals and the climate in which they live (DOK 4).

» Design the plans for an apparatus that applies the properties of light and sound to a technological design and demonstrates a specific purpose. Include a detailed labeled diagram (DOK 4).

» Examine the historical impact of the Hubble Space Telescope. Explain its strategic significance and the role that has been played by various agencies to maintain it as a viable resource. Identify positive and negative implications of allowing this telescope to become unusable. Based on your findings, make a judgment as to whether this resource should continue to receive funding (DOK 4).

LESSON 5.12
Work and Energy

NGSS Standards

  » MS-PS3-2

CCSS ELA Standards

  » RST.6-8.7
  » RST.6-8.9
  » WHST.6-8.1
  » WHST.6-8.7
  » WHST.6-8.8
  » WHST.6-8.9

Activities

  » Examine the relationship between productivity and leisure time. Research how these two concepts have been impacted by technological changes within our society over the past decade (DOK 1).

  » A complex mechanical system is made up of many subsystems composed of simple machines. Study a complex machine and determine which simple machines are used to create the complex machine. Then draw a diagram to demonstrate how they work together (DOK 2).

  » Suppose you are part of a local transportation advisory committee that is researching futuristic methods to reduce traffic congestion. Draft a presentation to pitch your ideas (DOK 3).

  » People have depended on machines for thousands of years to make their lives easier and more enjoyable. Prepare a timeline that will demonstrate the development of selected machines over time. Demonstrate the dependence of present-day machinery on the machine designs of the past (DOK 3).

  » Identify and conduct an experiment that tests the interactions of energy with matter, including changes of state and conservation of mass and energy (DOK 3).

  » Consider how the field of robotics aids in the exploration of places that are not comfortable for humans to enter, such as Antarctica and other planets.

Create a presentation in which you describe your findings and the derived benefits (DOK 3).

» Design and conduct an experiment in which you can calculate the work input, work output, efficiency, and mechanical advantage of a specific complex machine. Hypothesize as to ways in which any of these factors could be improved if this machine were used in different ways (DOK 4).

» Explore Rube Goldberg's website. Design a Rube Goldberg-type machine using at least three real simple machines that will solve an issue you or your family faces on a regular basis (DOK 4).

LESSON 5.13
Energy and Forces

NGSS Standards

- » MS-PS2-1
- » MS-PS2-2
- » MS-PS2-4
- » MS-PS2-5

CCSS ELA Standards

- » RST.6-8.2
- » WHST.6-8.2

Activities

- » Describe how the science of forces applies to the U.S. Space Program. Identify the forces needed to launch a rocket versus the forces involved in the re-entry process (DOK 1).
- » Demonstrate how energy forces have changed in each millennium since pre-historic times (DOK 1).
- » Study your home, school, or job site. Categorize the examples you find of mechanical, heat, chemical, electromagnetic, solar, wind, and/or nuclear energy. Create a description of how another type of energy might be more efficient for one example in at least three of the categories (DOK 2).
- » Study one of the major blackouts in recent history. Explain why and how it occurred. Describe engineers' efforts how to prevent similar reoccurrences (DOK 2).
- » Research a career in an energy-related field. Describe the types of work in which a person in this field engages. Learn about the training and certification needed to become qualified in one of these fields. Predict how these requirements might change over the next two decades (DOK 3).
- » Research the life of a scientist who has made important contributions to the field of energy and/or forces. Evaluate this person's contribution to his or her field, both at the time the discovery was made and in today's timeframe (DOK 3).

» Create a demonstration you could present to elementary students so they would understand the science of force. Relate this to everyday events that will help the students make the connection (DOK 4).

» Create a job description for a new Secretary of Energy Conservation. Include a detailed description of the ways in which that department could operate to make sure future generations have adequate energy supplies. Apply the concepts you have studied and researched to create this job position description (DOK 4).

LESSON 5.14
Air Pollution

NGSS Standards

- » MS-ESS3-3
- » MS-ESS3-4

CCSS ELA Standards

- » RST.6-8.1
- » RST.6-8.7
- » WHST.6-8.4

Activities

- » Identify the different causes of air pollution and demonstrate how the different pollutants affect human's health. Create a presentation to share with your class (DOK 1).
- » Consider how and why the Earth's ozone layer is thinning or disappearing in some areas. Create a presentation describing how the disappearing ozone layer could be harmful for the Earth. Include references (DOK 2).
- » Construct a digital or physical model of a wind turbine or a windmill. Prepare an explanation describing how the energy is captured and stored for future use (DOK 2).
- » Research a famous environmentalist. Create an informational brochure about the person and his or her contributions. Hypothesize as to how our world might be different had this individual not made this contribution (DOK 3).
- » Investigate what the factories and businesses in your local area do to reduce air pollution. Create a prioritized list identifying those that are the most successful and those that are the least successful in protecting air quality. Analyze and share commonalities found in green businesses. Create an advertisement for one of the green businesses that focuses attention on the information you have learned (DOK 3).
- » Wind power is a source of clean energy. Large areas of wind turbines generating electricity are called "wind farms." Research where wind farms are located in the United States and around the world. Mark the locations on a map. Study and report on environmental issues that exist and are addressed with

this resource. Cite evidence to support how these issues have impacted the development of this energy source (DOK 3).

» Geothermal power is a renewable energy source. Study the environmental impact of this renewable resource. Defend the statement, "Geothermal power is/is not a green energy source." Describe how and why different groups of people support or oppose this statement. Create a presentation to share your findings (DOK 4).

» Create a video that encourages people to change elements/activities of their lifestyles to decrease amounts of air pollution. Challenge people's personal reasons for resisting making lifestyle changes that could make progress in the elimination of air pollution. Identify compelling data in your presentation (DOK 4).

LESSON 5.15
Atmosphere

NGSS Standards

- » MS-ESS2-5
- » MS-ESS2-6
- » MS-ESS3-5

CCSS ELA Standards

- » RST.6-8.2
- » RST.6-8.7
- » RST.6-8.9

Activities

- » Study the effects of flying a plane at various altitudes. Create a chart to describe how atmospheric conditions, such as speed, fuel consumption, and safety, affect flying elements (DOK 1).
- » A number of respiratory diseases are connected to atmospheric conditions. Gather information related to several of these diseases and create a public health bulletin to alert people to the dangers (DOK 2).
- » Compare and contrast the ways in which the word "atmosphere" is used in ways other than to mean the atmosphere of the planet. Research the etymologies of the word. Find and describe as many related words as you can (DOK 2).
- » Research the use of alternative energy sources with and without the presence of gasoline engines and determine the degree to which such conveyances impact the atmosphere. In your presentation, include factors that may impact the degree to which these vehicles will be utilized. Make a prediction as to their future use based on your research and analysis about the viability of these vehicles (DOK 3).
- » Examine the developments in weather prediction that have occurred over the last 10 years, and predict what techniques might appear in the future to improve the predictability of weather forecasts. Select a presentation method and present to your class (DOK 3).

» Most rocketry and all spaceflight necessitate leaving Earth's atmosphere. Identify and predict how the problems they present might be overcome in your lifetime. Use your findings to create a persuasive piece in support of or against the viability of space travel (DOK 3).

» Study the conditions of contrast radiation, conduction, and convection as they appear in the atmosphere. Determine their long-term impact on mankind and the environment. Present your results in a position paper or presentation format of your choosing (DOK 4).

» Examine how hot air balloons have enhanced our understanding of the atmosphere. Design a future experiment in which such balloons might further impact this understanding. Include a rationale to support your ideas (DOK 4).

LESSON 5.16
Diversity in Environments

NGSS Standard

 » MS-LS2-5

CCSS ELA Standards

 » RST.6-8.7
 » RST.6-8.9
 » WHST.6-8.1
 » WHST.6-8.9

Activities

 » Study and report on the process that creates state and national parks and preserves (DOK 1).
 » Study a local environment and describe the relationships among the organisms present in the habitat (DOK 1).
 » Investigate an ecosystem and compare and contrast the density-dependent and density-independent factors present within the system. Create a campaign to make people aware of this situation (DOK 2).
 » Choose a biome and an ecosystem within this biome. Investigate this area and learn about the future of its stability. Predict what would happen to this ecosystem's stability if its carrying capacities were exceeded (DOK 3).
 » Present the factors that influence the size and stability of populations within an ecosystem by distinguishing between and interpreting graphs of a j-curve, boom or bust curve, and s-curve to describe trends (DOK 3).
 » Find evidence to develop a logical argument that supports a pro- or con- position regarding the issue of keeping the Antarctic region open only for scientific research and closed to tourist visits (DOK 3).
 » Investigate a biome. Describe the adaptive, competitive, and survival potential characteristics of a group of organisms in this environment (e.g., plants and animals of a forest or prairie; DOK 3).
 » Compare and contrast desert regions of the world. Create a presentation comparing a desert nearest to your home with another desert. Consider how each desert influences social and/or political dynamics of the region (DOK 4).

LESSON 5.17
Earth Science

NGSS Standards

- » MS-ESS2-4
- » MS-ESS2-3
- » MS-ESS3-2

CCSS ELA Standards

- » RST.6-8.1
- » RST.6-8.9
- » WHST.6-8.2

Activities

- » Describe the natural cycles of Earth's land, water, and atmospheric systems in the following ways (DOK 1):
  - ♦ explain erosion and weathering,
  - ♦ discuss the effect of erosion and weathering, and
  - ♦ present examples of erosion and weathering that have shaped our natural landscape.

- » Identify and describe the natural cycles of Earth's land, water, and atmospheric systems in the following ways (DOK 2):
  - ♦ explain and summarize the water cycle,
  - ♦ explain weathering patterns based on atmospheric cycles, and
  - ♦ record and describe daily local atmospheric conditions over a given time period.

- » Create a touring itinerary lasting several weeks that would allow travelers to view and compare the many features we are studying in this unit during a trip. Use any conventional means of travel you choose to make the most feature-filled itinerary possible (DOK 2).
- » Study and report on methods used to predict earthquakes and/or volcanic eruptions (DOK 2).

» Identify and report on the impact of occurrences of phenomena such as earthquakes, volcanoes, weathering, and erosion on the Earth's landscape (DOK 2).

» Identify and report on the impact of occurrences of phenomena such as earthquakes, volcanoes, weathering, and erosion on the Earth's landscape and on its people. How do these phenomena impact the inhabitants of the area from a survival as well as an emotional perspective (DOK 3)?

» Study rock formations that may be found in the area in which you currently live or have lived in the past. Apply what you know about rocks and Earth formations to assess the stages of geologic growth your area has gone through over the past several thousand years. Include descriptions of any personal experiences you have had that support your conjectures (DOK 3).

» Create a WebQuest about several women who have made important contributions to an area related to Earth science. In your project, describe social or political obstacles these women faced in their crusades (DOK 4).

LESSON 5.18

Ecosystems

NGSS Standards

- » MS-LS2-4
- » MS-LS2-5
- » HS-LS2-7

CCSS ELA Standards

- » RST.6-8.2
- » RST.6-8.9
- » WHST.9-10.1
- » WHST.9-10.4

Activities

- » Research and describe what homeowners in high wildfire danger areas should do to proactively protect their homes (DOK 1).
- » Research and describe what homeowners in high wildfire danger areas should do to proactively protect their homes. With this information, design a campaign to inform residents of the dangers and methods to protect their homes (DOK 2).
- » Contact your state's park association to become familiar with its efforts to save the parks in your state from ruined ecosystems. Report on the effects of these efforts (DOK 2).
- » Research the impact of highways on the local ecosystems. Identify and present ways in which civil engineers attempt to avoid negative impacts on the ecosystem (DOK 2).
- » Identify ways to involve others in the preservation of ecosystems. Create an ad campaign to engage the target audiences in these efforts (DOK 3).
- » Study the misunderstanding regarding the practice of controlling wildfires by setting them intentionally. Develop a logical argument supporting the scientific process. Construct a persuasive argument in which you attempt to clarify the misunderstanding (DOK 3).
- » Report on the short- and long-term effects of a major oil spill. Assess the ways in which such an event impacts several ecosystems simultaneously. In your

discussion, address efforts and obstacles that have taken place with attempts to prevent reoccurrences of oil spills in the past. Include methods that may prevent future detrimental impacts to ecosystems (DOK 4).

» Investigate the pollution tolerance levels of various organisms found in a location in your area. Create an awareness campaign to influence perpetrators of pollution to become more aware of and responsive to the negative effects of their waste materials. Include possible political support or constraints associated with these efforts (DOK 4).

LESSON 5.19
Environment

NGSS Standards

» MS-ESS3-3
» MS-ESS3-4

CCSS ELA Standards

» RST.6-8.2
» RST.6-8.9
» WHST.6-8.1
» WHST.6-8.2

Activities

» Research a famous environmentalist. Create an informational brochure about the person and his or her contributions (DOK 1).

» Research and report on the advantages and challenges associated with composting. Create a presentation that will convince others (DOK 2).

» Design an original ad campaign that promotes the green movement. Include a slogan and a visual representation. Prepare a presentation to share your campaign (DOK 2).

» Research how other towns and cities across the nation recycle. Identify the "greenest" city in the U.S. Examine and describe what gives the city this distinction and what it does differently than your hometown (DOK 3).

» Global warming remains a widely debated topic. Research the topic. Is global warming an imminent world threat? What actions do you believe should be taken to address the global warming issue? (DOK 3)

» Imagine the year 2050. What do you think life will be like? Describe ways in which it might be different from life today from an environmental perspective. Provide rationale that considers expected transformations based on past occurrences to support your claims (DOK 4).

» Pretend you are the planet. Citing facts, create a diagnosis regarding your current "state of health." Include facts to support your statement of health. Design a prescriptive intervention plan for the humans to follow to bring you back to good health. Prioritize the actions in your plan (DOK 4).

» Create a comic strip with a plotline about recycling and keeping the planet clean. Invent a "green" superhero to star in the story and a villain who doesn't care about the environment. Attempt to make the villain learn a lesson by the end of the story (DOK 4).

LESSON 5.20
Volcanoes

NGSS Standard

» MS-ESS2-3

CCSS ELA Standards

» RST.6-8.1
» RST.6-8.7
» WHST.6-8.7
» WHST.6-8.8
» WHST.6-8.9

Activities

» Study myths and folk stories, as well as anthropological accounts of ways in which the presence of volcanoes have impacted the lives and religious beliefs of peoples living in the shadow of potentially live volcanoes. Report your findings in a project of your choice (DOK 1).

» Investigate ways in which modern science has improved the accuracy of predicting volcanic activity. Study traditional methods of prediction, including myth and folktale (DOK 1).

» "Lahar" is an Indonesian term for a particularly deadly type of volcanic mudflow. Research lahars from two separate eruptions and explain how lahars are different from typical volcanic flow (DOK 2).

» Investigate several websites devoted to the topic of volcanoes. Choose a subtopic about which you know very little, and gather information so you can present it in an interesting way to an appropriate audience (DOK 2).

» Using your knowledge of Latin roots, try to discover the meaning of the term "pneumonoultramicroscopicsilicovolcanoconiosis." Invent several similarly complex terms to explain other aspects of volcanic activity (DOK 2).

» Read fictional and nonfictional accounts of volcanic eruptions during several time periods. Analyze the degree to which each treatment gives factual information and write a comparative analysis (DOK 3).

» Discover ways and locations in which volcanic activity has created landmasses and ways in which it has made the landmasses disappear. Based on what you learn and current volcanic activity, predict the general location where new landmasses might form within the next 50 years. Provide specific reasons for your predictions (DOK 4).

» Investigate active volcanoes in the world. Identify one that is most likely to erupt. Calculate the potential impact it would cause if it was to erupt. Create a presentation that teaches students about volcanoes and demonstrates steps people can take in the different areas to protect themselves from potential dangers (DOK 4).

LESSON 5.21
Water Pollution

NGSS Standard

» MS-ESS2-4

CCSS ELA Standards

» RST.6-8.1
» RST.6-8.7
» WHST.6-8.7
» WHST.6-8.8
» WHST.6-8.9

Activities

» Draw a detailed picture of your favorite water habitat. Include all of the plants and animals that live in that habitat and label them. Identify the threats to this wildlife based on pollution in the area (DOK 1).

» How does water pollution affect the fishing industry? Which states are most significantly impacted? Locate these states on a map or globe and provide examples of the impact of pollution on fishing. Create a presentation to share your findings (DOK 2).

» Identify where the world's fresh water supplies can be found and in what amounts. Describe how those amounts have changed over time. Display this data in a graphic presentation (DOK 2).

» Learn about the different causes of water pollution and how water pollution affects our health. Create a presentation to share with your class (DOK 2).

» Study the science behind wind turbines, windmills, and wind energy windmills. Create a presentation describing how the energy is captured and utilized and their possible impact on water pollution (DOK 3).

» Research a famous environmentalist whose work is specific to the area in which you live or in which you have lived in the past. Create a presentation in which you introduce this person's efforts and contributions. Include any personal connections you many have to this cause (DOK 3).

» Research and discuss the importance of water conservation. Write an editorial explaining the impact on our world if conservation measures were not taken.

Cite evidence of the successes and challenges from past and present conservation efforts (DOK 3).

» Create a project in which you explain how polluted water harms people and animals. Include the ethical dilemma of man's responsibility toward nature and economic and societal factors that interfere with efforts to protect lives (DOK 4).

LESSON 5.22
Water Quality and Ecology

NGSS Standard

» MS-ESS2-4

CCSS ELA Standards

» RST.6-8.7
» RST.6-8.9.
» WHST.6-8.7
» WHST.6-8.8
» WHST.6-8.9

Activities

» Investigate several careers that involve water. Identify the qualifications, training, and job descriptions needed for each (DOK 1).

» Describe and illustrate the cycling of water through the Earth's systems (DOK 1).

» Investigate the water shortage of a country or area of your choice. Design a list of efforts being made to solve one or more of the problems resulting from the shortage (DOK 2).

» Compare and contrast the effects of water pollution to other types of pollution. Identify and describe the elements all types of pollution have in common (DOK 2).

» Describe water use trends over time for your state. Connect those trends to local and national events. Using what you notice, predict future trends (DOK 3).

» Study the effects of various water treatment components at your local water treatment location. Identify and examine possible threats to the water's drinking safety. Report on recommendations and steps being implemented to ensure a continuously safe water supply for your community (DOK 3).

» Study and evaluate the companies that claim to manufacture purified water. Learn about and describe the methods used to create their products. Investigate and report on the differences in these methods (DOK 3).

» Project the future water needs for your geographic area. Analyze the challenges of providing water that is good enough for human consumption and plant and animal needs. Create plans for a water conservation program that will encourage people to conserve water at the present time to provide for future needs. Predict obstacles that would likely surface in these efforts (DOK 4).

LESSON 5.23
Weathering and Erosion

NGSS Standard

» MS-ESS2-2

CCSS ELA Standards

» RST.6-8.1
» RST.6-8.7
» RST.6-8.9
» WHST.6-8.4

Activities

» Locate and describe active glaciers. In your project, discuss how glaciers have formed in different areas (DOK 1).

» Describe the power that nature holds over humans. Include a discussion on how natural forces always dominate in the long run (DOK 2).

» Study and report on forest fire burn sites and prediction techniques that show how scientists have learned from past experiences to minimize future damage from burn site erosion (DOK 2).

» Investigate the political and economic realities in areas of great famine when relief supplies rarely reach the people who need relief. Report on reasons this occurs and attempts organizations use to bypass these barriers (DOK 3).

» Identify and prioritize the issues regarding Earth sciences that you believe the U.S. Congress should address in order to minimize the long-term effects of weathering and erosion in a specific area. Describe your rationale in your project (DOK 3).

» Compare standards of living in several different regions of the world and determine how different soil types have influenced these standards (DOK 3).

» Survey sites near your living area in which weathering and erosion effects are clearly visible. Investigate others' attempts to improve the situation. Evaluate the degree to which those efforts have been effective. Create a message to share with the community on how their awareness of these efforts might help to avoid further damage (DOK 4).

» Synthesize earthquake data and prediction techniques to show how science has learned from past experience how to minimize future damage from earthquakes. Compare methods used in different parts of the world. Determine the most accurate measure based on your data findings and hypothesize as to why those measures are not universally used (DOK 4).

LESSON 5.24
Wildlife Conservation

NGSS Standard

» MS-ESS3-3

CCSS ELA Standards

» RST.6-8.1
» RST.6-8.7
» WHST.6-8.7
» WHST.6-8.8
» WHST.6-8.9

Activities

» Investigate and describe the pros and cons of developing North American oil reserves as a way to combat dependence on oil from the Middle East (DOK 1).

» Study the life of a famous conservationist. Imagine how his or her struggle in modern times might be different. Describe your findings in a way that would inspire present-day conservationists (DOK 2).

» Research the work of zoos in preventing the extinction of species of animals. Design an infomercial to increase public awareness about the importance of the work of zoos (DOK 2).

» Over time, theories regarding how certain species disappeared change. Select one species and investigate the various theories about what caused its disappearance. If you are dissatisfied with present theories, provide another viable option (DOK 3).

» Study the vacant areas near your community that are presently being developed into home or business areas. Calculate the impact of these areas on species indigenous to your area. Create a campaign to share the information with local citizens (DOK 3).

» Research how shrinking habitats for different species of animals impacts their endangered status. Select one endangered species and describe its plight. Investigate ways for that species to find sustenance some place other than its own natural habitat (DOK 3).

» Investigate a species that was once endangered and has since been removed from that list. Become familiar with and report on the strategies used to renew that species' viability (DOK 3).

» Select an endangered species and prepare reference materials to use in a debate in which you extrapolate on the relative merits of keeping a particular species alive (DOK 4).

LESSON 5.25
Technology in the Sciences

ISTE Standard

» NT.K-12.2 Social, Ethical, and Human Issues

CCSS ELA Standards

» RST.6-8.2
» RST.6-8.8
» RST.6-8.9
» WHST.6-8.6

Activities

» Describe the effects of "outsourcing" to foreign countries the manufacturing of products historically made in the United States. How do companies compensate for lower levels of technology in emerging countries (DOK 1)?

» Research two careers in technological fields that you may be interested in pursuing as an adult. Identify and consider the qualifications and training needed for the jobs. Write a description of the tasks involved in a typical day of work in that field (DOK 1).

» Examine current technology used in air traffic control. Develop a list of criteria that could be used to evaluate a specific airport's current system (DOK 2).

» Research on the emergence of genetic engineering. Prepare a presentation in which you describe or demonstrate how it is used in agriculture to create new or better types of food (DOK 2).

» Research and analyze how nanotechnology is used in the field of health care. Investigate how this type of technology is impacting surgical procedures (DOK 3).

» Interview a senior citizen and a younger adult regarding the type of entertainment that existed when he or she was a child. Compare this to present forms that are available to you. Create a visual and a description of how entertainment has evolved overtime. Predict the ways in which the technology of entertainment might differ for your own children (DOK 3).

» Compare and contrast the effectiveness of the tools used by archeologists in the field in present times and those used 50 years ago. Create a presentation of your findings (DOK 3).

» Investigate how current technology is used to forecast an environmental catastrophe such as an earthquake, drought, or hurricane. Identify a major catastrophe caused by nature during the past two decades. Investigate the identified causes and describe technological advancements put into place since the accident. Describe what groups were responsible for the proposed advancements and the controversies surrounding the reconstruction efforts (DOK 4).

6

Special Areas and Electives Extension Lessons

Introduction

The extension lessons in this chapter provide special areas and elective teachers opportunities to further explore the elements within their field of study. These extension lessons allow students to develop their critical and creative thinking processes and deepen their understanding of the selected field of study. The extensions have been divided into the following categories: art, band and orchestra, dance and physical education, general music, and world languages.

Connections to Standards

Standards have been provided in both the content area, when applicable, and the CCSS for ELA (NGA & CCSSO, 2010a). Individual districts and states have specific standards, yet for continuity of interpretation, the standards that have been selected are national standards. Standards addressed in this chapter include:

> National Core Arts Standards (National Coalition for Core Arts Standards [NCCAS], 2014): Lessons 6.1–6.15

> SHAPE America's National Standards for K–12 Physical Education (2013): Lesson 6.16–6.17

> World-Readiness Standards for Learning Languages (The National Standards Collaborative Board, 2015): Lessons 6.18–6.19

Sample Lesson

In the sample lesson for this chapter, the students are exploring the area of characterization in theatre arts. The skills an actor needs to be successful in school and in the world are the same skills students need to be successful in theatre. One needs to be able to listen, think on one's feet, think critically, create and innovate, as well as exhibit meaningful communication, and work well in a team atmosphere, despite when conflicts arise. In this sample, the teacher has chosen to engage students with extension lessons after the lesson has been presented, however, you may feel that these lesson exercises can be utilized anytime throughout the acting and directing process to help students connect with their character. The extensions expand students' understandings by providing options of increased complexity.

Using the extension lesson, "Theatre Arts: Characterization," the student is asked to use text evidence to provide a detailed description of a given character in DOK Level 1. This activity provides a very basic level of complexity while still connecting the students to the concept of characterization and the beginning stages of examining a character. DOK Levels 2 and 3 have the students delve deeper into their character as the students create a persona in relationship to the other characters. DOK Level 4 synthesizes the information provided along with the exercises in which the students have engaged. This combination allows them to develop a deep understanding of their character—how he or she thinks and reacts, and his or her place in the world of the play. This level of complexity requires higher levels of creativity, critical thinking, and deeper reasoning skills. Utilizing this process of scaffolding the lesson to include in-class instruction, students engage, explore, and then further their study with one or more activities from the extension lesson. Students can gain a deeper understanding of the text, the author, and their character, thus making their learning more meaningful.

Sample Theatre Arts Lesson

The ability to analyze a text, utilize the details, and draw conclusions about the authors' intention is pertinent in theatre, language arts, music, and art. Being able to ascertain this intention as well as create the intended message through one's craft is vital. In theatre, this is accomplished through character and script development. This lesson focuses on the art of characterization. The students begin with a visualization exercise, then work on developing character types using improvisation. The extension lesson titled, "Theatre Arts: Characterization" will guide the students deeper into text and the discovery of their characters.

In this lesson, students are asked to participate in an exercise where they rely on images that depict characterization. They go through improvisational activities to develop their characterization skills and teamwork. Finally, the students conduct a script analysis to further understand and develop their character. As students work through this series of lessons they are provided with the extension lesson "Theatre Arts: Characterization." The teacher guides students in exploring depth and complexity levels within the extension lesson. Student performance on class activities, in reflection, and in discussion, provide the data used to determine the appropriate DOK level needed to provide challenge.

Essential Questions
1. How do visual images and visual depictions shape character development?
2. How does improvisational work develop characterization?
3. How important is script analysis in development of a character?

Lesson Focus
To provide students with the strategies necessary to develop their own characterizations

Objectives
Students will:
1. analyze the physical depictions of a character in images to devise characterization;
2. develop, communicate, and sustain a character in improvisation;
3. analyze the physical, emotional, and social dimensions of characters provided by the text evidence in a script; and
4. closely read the script, notice details, and infer how these details develop the characterization of a character.

CCSS ELA Standards
o   RL.6.3
o   RL.7.3
o   RL.8.3
o   RL.9-10.3

NCCAS Standards for Theatre
o   Anchor Standards 1–5

Key Vocabulary
o   Characterization, improvisation, visualization

Materials
o   Script
o   Pictures of characters

Lesson Frame: Parts 1, 2, and 3
Part 1: Choose a play that may be somewhat familiar to your students, such as *A Midsummer Night's Dream*. Download images of the characters from the play, yet have them be ambiguous enough to not be immediately recognizable. Give every student a picture without identifying the subject. Have each student write on the backside of the picture or on another piece of paper in response to the following: Who is the person in the picture? Where do they

live? What do they fear? What is their relationship with their family? What's their philosophy of life?

Alternative exercise: You may also select many pictures of the same character from different productions and have the students answer the same questions and then discuss the images as a development of characterization.

Think/Pair/Share with table team. Have students view the images collectively, either in a small group or as an entire class. With table teammates, students share what they observed in each image. Give examples of how the details of each image tell the story of an entire character or play. As a team, have each group determine the character or characters and the title of the play. Each team will share its character choice/s and the title of the play with the class along with its supporting evidence.

Part 2: Improvisation is a great way to teach students about the perspective of others, the acceptance of others' ideas, and how to collaborate to create better ideas. The following are improvisational activities that may be done in partners or small groups. They are designed to help students focus on the qualities that define characterization.

- o **Three Lines:** The goal of this exercise is to force the actors into making strong choices as quickly as possible. The actors are placed in pairs and given a sense of dialogue. The actors make a strong character choice (physical, vocal, emotional, motivationally, and point of view) as well as the environment and the setting or platform of the scene. They then begin their scene and are broken off after three lines each. Once these three lines of dialogue are complete, the actors take their characterizations and begin again with a new scene. At the completion of this, they reflect on their choices.

- o **Character Swap:** Students pair off and are handed a dialogue idea, they are instructed to make a strong character choice (physical, vocal, emotional, motivationally, and point of view) before beginning. The scene begins and must continue until both of the actors have clearly personified their character so that classmates can know them. At this time the roles are switched. However, students must play their new character precisely how their opponent had previously. The goal of this exercise is to train the actors to actively participate, listen, and respond to their surroundings and other characters.

- o **Opposite Characters:** Provide a scenario or a scene from a script. Two players stand opposite one another and are surrounded by a team of coaches. The goal of this exercise is to have the actors focus on the choices of their opponent and then to do the exact opposite. The coaches are to direct the players and help them focus on the following character traits: voice, tone, pitch, mannerisms, body movement, and perhaps social class, culture, dialect, or accent.

- o **Communal monologue (two options):**
  - Students stand in a circle and one in the middle. The student in the center recites a monologue, as the students in the circle share emotions such as anger, sadness, elation. The goal is to have the team try to coach the actor into making clear and precise choices.
  - A student begins the monologue. At any moment, another student may enter the circle and continue the monologue, but must alter the characterization. This process continues until all who want to participate have had the opportunity to do so. The goal is that the actors can develop their ideas of characterization from their peers.

Part 3: Students begin by using script analysis to develop characterization. Students participate in a visualization exercise by journaling in response to the following questions: Who is your character? What does the script explicitly say? What is their relationship to others in the script? What do other characters say about them? What does the script tell about what they see, smell, feel, and think? How do they react to situations? What does the script infer about what type of person they are?

Closure: The students draw a picture or create a collage of pictures that helps them visualize their characterization of their character based on their journal entries.

Extension Lesson

As students develop their reflection, the teacher will guide students to the DOK level of extension appropriate to meet their challenge needs. Students are provided time to work on their extension lesson selection each day as the lesson series progresses. In this manner, students are provided with the additional challenge needed and given an opportunity to extend their thinking and practice with self-regulating their work time.

LESSON 6.1
Instructional Music

NCCAS Standards for Music

» Anchor Standards 1-4

CCSS ELA Standards

» CCRA.R.7
» CCRA.W.1
» CCRA.W.6

Activities

» Create a chart highlighting the styles and works of composers for the instrument you are learning to play. Choose composers from several different time periods for your study.

» Investigate the life and work of a composer whose music appeals to you, and compare and contrast it to the work of a composer from the same time period whose music you do not enjoy (DOK 2).

» Research the life of a successful professional musician you admire. Develop a list of interview questions that would help you understand him as a musician and a person. If possible, find a way to contact and interview that person (DOK 2).

» Study the life of a composer you admire greatly. Draw conclusions as to how the events of his or her life are reflected in the music this person composed (DOK 3).

» Investigate the lives and works of famous musical prodigies. Describe the events and circumstances that influenced their development and success as composers or performers. Identify the elements that most likely led to their success (DOK 3).

» Research the styles several conductors use for different types of instrumental groups. Consider the types of challenges these conductors might experience in their work and how the different type of instrumental groups may influence those challenges (DOK 3).

» Create and defend a theory of how to become a successful professional musician. Draw upon societal, economic, and/or political factors (DOK 4).

» Compose a piece of music and perform it in an ensemble (DOK 4).

LESSON 6.2
Music Styles

NCCAS Standards for Music

- » Anchor Standards 1-4
- » Anchor Standards 6-9
- » Anchor Standard 11

CCSS ELA Standards

- » CCRA.R.8
- » CCRA.W.2
- » CCRA.W.6

Activities

- » Study the life story of a musical artist you admire. Through research, identify how experiences impacted the person's music (DOK 1).
- » Listen to examples of music by a composer/songwriter we have studied. Identify the elements this person's works have in common. Describe the differences as well (DOK 2).
- » Artistic works evolve over time. Select an artist you admire and study how his or her work changed over time. Present possible influences that account for the change (DOK 2).
- » Compose a short a piece of music and play it on both a traditional and nontraditional instrument (DOK 3).
- » Research how music styles have changed over the decades within a given time period. Examine how society has influenced these changes (DOK 3)
- » Create a song or piece using elements from a style of music we are studying (DOK 3).
- » Rewrite a piece of music from the past so it would appeal to several types of contemporary groups. Provide a rationale for the elements changed or modified (DOK 4).
- » Investigate the connections between clothing styles and kinds of music being played and sung during an era of time. Draw a conclusion on the effects of one element on the other (DOK 4).

LESSON 6.3
Study of Music

NCCAS Standards for Music

» Anchor Standards 1-4
» Anchor Standards 6-9
» Anchor Standard 11

CCSS ELA Standards

» CCRA.R.7
» CCRA.R.8
» CCRA.W.6
» CCRA.W.8

Activities

» The basic elements of music are described as: melody, harmony, tone, timbre, form, tempo or rhythm, and dynamics. Examine a piece of music that pleases you and describe how the elements are used in that selection (DOK 1).

» Identify a favorite musician who has made a tremendous impact in the field. Collect and display information that informs others on this person's contributions to the world (DOK 1).

» Examine a score from a larger work, such as a symphony or other orchestral piece. Listen to at least two different performances of that piece as you follow along in the score. Compare and contrast the versions of the piece (DOK 2).

» Design and create an instructional video that teaches and demonstrates the elements of music. Identify your audience and include objectives (DOK 2).

» Study the music of another culture. Create a way to demonstrate the similarities and differences in the music of your culture and the one chosen. Cite evidence demonstrating how each country or region's music illustrates or reflects the cultural and/or historical influences that have been applied to them (DOK 3).

» Examine several performances of the same piece of contemporary music, either instrumental or vocal. Determine ways in which those performances are dissimilar and decide which version you prefer. Identify those differences and explain your preference in each difference you identify (DOK 3).

» Select a favorite piece or musical score of one of the artists you have studied. Critique the piece by utilizing the following elements of music: beat and meter, harmony, tone, melody, timbre, form, tempo, and rhythm of a specific movement (DOK 3).

» Research various careers in music. Find a person already working in the field and "shadow" that person at work. Write a blog or journal entry chronicling the experience. Include your observations and your reactions to the events you encounter, along with how your desire to become a professional in that field is influenced by the mentorship (DOK 4).

LESSON 6.4
Vocal Music

NCCAS Standards for Music

» Anchor Standards 1–4, 6–9, 11

CCSS ELA Standards

» CCRA.R.7
» CCRA.R.8
» CCRA.W.2
» CCRA.W.7

Activities

» Identify the elements contained within songs of a particular genre (DOK 1).
» Describe similarities and differences between the use of poetic language and musical language (DOK 2).
» Connect (either in person or online) with musicians who are producing and publishing new vocal music. Provide a transcript of your collaboration with the musician (DOK 2).
» Listen to several examples of choral groups performing the same composition, such as "Carmina Burama" by Carl Orff. Create an auditory experience for your musical classmates to demonstrate several differences between the various recordings. Provide for your audience to participate by discussing their perceptions and preferences and giving reasons for their choices (DOK 2).
» Develop a logical argument to present how a different interpretation, regarding dynamics, phrasing, or other interpretive elements, might improve the performance of a particular section or piece of music. Include both the present arrangement and your own in the demonstration (DOK 3).
» Examine a particular form of classical music, such as the Requiems of Mozart and Brahms. Compare the lyrics and phrasing of one you choose to other Requiem masses you find by other composers. Present what you have discovered about the elements Requiem masses have in common (DOK 3).
» Compose an original score to accompany a staged reading of a fairytale. Your selection can be a compilation of original music or of prerecorded music.

Your music selection must highlight the plot and the development of the characters (DOK 4).

» Create a lesson for younger elementary age students to instruct them about vocal music. Compose a piece of music that you will then teach and rehearse with them. Record the final performance and submit the original score (DOK 4).

LESSON 6.5
Band

NCCAS Standards for Music

» Anchor Standards 1–4, 6–9, 11

CCSS ELA Standards

» CCRA.R.7
» CCRA.R.8
» CCRA.W.2

Activities

» Create a presentation that teaches elementary students about the instruments used in band. Include a brief description of the history of the instruments (DOK 1).

» Locate and describe 5–10 instruments that are not commonly included in school bands. What are possible reasons for the lack of use of these instruments (DOK 1)?

» Locate a piece of music from the Music Division Site of the Library of Congress. Identify an historical event from the time period chosen and examine how it is depicted in the specific piece of music (DOK 2).

» Research the history of the band instrument you play to learn how the instrument has been used over time (DOK 2).

» Examine the methods that are currently used to teach one how to play a musical instrument. Evaluate their effectiveness. Rank order the methods identified through your research. Select a preferred method and explain why you prefer it (DOK 3).

» On September 27, 1974, the Music Division of the Library of Congress recreated a typical concert of brass band and vocal music from mid-19th-century America. That concert became the starting-point for *Band Music From the Civil War Era*, an online collection that brings together musical scores, recordings, photographs, and essays documenting an important but insufficiently explored part of the American musical past. Using this resource, create a WebQuest that will allow others to learn and explore from this era.

Your WebQuest must include an introduction, task, process, evaluation, and teacher page (DOK 3).

» Select a piece of music. Arrange it for your instrument and one other. Make a recording of the arrangement to share with your bandmates (DOK 3).

» Identify several common marches, such as those written by John Phillips Sousa. Describe the pieces relative to the time period when they were written. Discuss social or political factors present during the time and speculate as to their influence on the pieces. What elements of this musical composition format align with the political factors you identified (DOK 4)?

LESSON 6.6

Instrumental Music: Digital Connections

NCCAS Standards for Music

» Anchor Standards 1–9, 11

CCSS ELA Standards

» CCRA.R.7
» CCRA.R.8
» CCRA.W.2
» CCRA.W.6

Activities

» MIDI (Musical Instrument Digital Interface) productions are controlled by several companies, one in Los Angeles and another in Tokyo. Research the controls they maintain and determine the cost to MIDI technicians to use their digital systems legally (DOK 1).
» Study the development of MIDI, which allows multiple instruments to be played from a single controller. This process previously would have required the use of several controllers, all working simultaneously. Create a presentation describing this system (DOK 1).
» Connect online with musicians who blog. Follow their postings and report on your findings (DOK 2).
» Demonstrate how MIDI delivers music in the following categories: notation, pitch, velocity, control volume, vibrato, audio panning, cues, and clock signals that set and synchronize tempo between multiple devices (DOK 2).
» Investigate and describe the history and developments of the MIDI systems and its uses. How might those changes impact music production in the world (DOK 3)?
» Locate a video or photos demonstrating the conductor's gestures for meter, tempo, dynamics, entrances, cutoffs, and phrasing to elicit expressive playing of musical instruments with the recording of a piece of music. Identify each gesture and provide the conductor's intent (DOK 3).

» Consider and discuss impacts on musical careers with the continued advancement of MIDI techniques. What adaptations have current musicians needed to make to remain viable in the field (DOK 4)?

» MIDI can mimic many instruments. Create a musical montage as a quiz for your classmates to determine their ease in distinguishing between the MIDI sounds and those created by actual instruments played by living musicians (DOK 4).

LESSON 6.7
Instrumental Music

NCCAS Standards for Music

»   Anchor Standards 1–4, 6–9, 11

CCSS ELA Standards

»   CCRA.R.7
»   CCRA.R.8
»   CCRA.W.1
»   CCRA.W.8

Activities

»   Identify the symbols of musical shorthand used by composers regarding pace, volume, and other dynamics of performing a specific piece of music. Design a presentation that explains them to the other members of the performance group as they are beginning to learn a new piece of music (DOK 1).

»   Research and then report on how to avoid hearing loss for the musicians involved in the performance of loud or bombastic music (DOK 1).

»   In a written essay, or other format, explain the physical health issues that can arise by not taking care of the cleanliness of a musical instrument. Consider both the instrument and its player. Create a method of delivering the information so behaviors will change for healthier outcomes (DOK 2).

»   Survey your classmates to learn why they chose the instruments they play. Create a digital graph depicting the reasons. Be creative (DOK 2).

»   Gather information regarding dangers of prolonged exposure to loud music. Create a chart that compares the decibel levels of various performance settings (DOK 2).

»   Examine a particular form of classical music, such as Mozart Requiem in D Minor, Brahams, or others, and locate and explain the similarities and differences between the pieces (DOK 2).

»   Examine a particular form of classical music, such as Mozart's Requiem in D Minor, Brahams, or others. Explain the similarities and differences between two examples. Create a demonstration wherein a group of your classmates compare and contrast the differences between a Requiem you explained and one they are hearing for the first time (DOK 3).

» Compose an arrangement and record it on the MIDI. Then present the final piece along with the score for peer evaluation (DOK 4).

LESSON 6.8
Orchestra

NCCAS Standards for Music

» Anchor Standards 1–11

CCSS ELA Standards

» CCRA.R.7
» CCRA.R.8
» CCRA.W.2

Activities

» Locate and describe an instrument that has currently less of a role in orchestral music than in previous centuries. Explain possible reasons for that situation (DOK 1).

» Examine several historic events about which orchestral pieces have been written such as Tchaikovsky's 1812 Overture. Identify and play a recording of selected parts of the piece. Analyze and explain how that event is depicted in that specific piece of music (DOK 2).

» Create a presentation that teaches elementary students about the instruments used in orchestra. Include a demonstration of the instruments and provide the history of the instruments (DOK 2).

» Examine the history of the instrument you play to determine how the instrument has changed over time. Why might these changes have occurred? Create a visual to illustrate any changes you think should be made in your instrument (DOK 3).

» Create a new or innovative way to teach interested persons how to play your musical instrument. Try out your method with a group of people. Get feedback from them about how to refine your method (DOK 3).

» Identify and describe five instruments not commonly found in a school orchestra. Research and identify possible reasons for the lack of use. Base your reasoning on evidence from your research (DOK 3).

» Select a piece of music to arrange for your orchestra and create and make a recording of the arrangement to share with your orchestra-mates and others. Then rearrange it for other solo instruments (DOK 4).

» Compose a piece for your orchestra. Record it being played by an ensemble of musicians you know. Ask the orchestra director to allow it to be auditioned before the orchestra in which you play (DOK 4).

LESSON 6.9
Art Fantasy Figures

NCCAS Standards for Visual Arts

» Anchor Standards 1–11

CCSS ELA Standard

» CCRA.R.7

Activities

» Create a presentation in which you identify and describe common traits of fantasy figures. Discuss what makes them appealing in the arts (DOK 1).

» Write and illustrate a storybook using a selected fantasy figure as the antagonist or protagonist. Set the story in the figure's fantasy world (DOK 2).

» Create a drawing and/or painting of a fantasy character. Create its history and a fantasy world in which the character can live (DOK 3).

» Study gargoyles and their qualities. Then invent a fantasy character in this format and place your character into a visual story (DOK 3).

» Create a journal chronicle or a comic book script of a selected fantasy character in which you depict adventures in their fantasy world (DOK 3).

» Critique a poem, book, or movie in which a fantasy figure is the main character. Discuss if you would change anything in the story, and if so, what elements (DOK 3).

» Design and animate a selected fantasy figure using clay animation. In your presentation, explain its relevance on the times and what you believe the figure represents within this context (DOK 4).

» Create a presentation in which you provide an overview of the evolution of fantasy figures in popular media. Include a discussion on why these figures prevail over the years and speculate as to the appeal and intrigue they have for audiences (DOK 4).

LESSON 6.10
Influences in Art

NCCAS Standards for Visual Arts

» Anchor Standard 1, 7–9, 11

CCSS ELA Standards

» CCRA.R.8
» CCRA.W.1
» CCRA.W.7

Activities

» Design a presentation that teaches students the basic elements of art: line, shape, form, space, texture, and color, including hue, value, and intensity (DOK 1).

» Select a country or civilization of your choice. Investigate and report on the importance artists had in the social, political, and economic development of that country or civilization (DOK 1).

» Identify a favorite artist. Create some work 'in the style of" that artist. Explain how that person's work influenced your own creation (DOK 2).

» Examine an artist's use of subjects, themes, and symbols in his or her work. In your project, infer the artist's intended meaning in his or her artwork. Provide evidence that supports your reasoning (DOK 3).

» Examine a piece of art. Assess the selected media, techniques, and processes the artist used. Analyze what makes these effective in communicating their ideas in this particular piece. Reflect upon the effectiveness of their choices (DOK 3).

» Investigate and describe how the work of a specific artist changed over time. Create a project in which you include visuals and reference the elements of art. Hypothesize as to the reasons for some of these changes (DOK 3).

» Analyze the factors of time and place (such as climate, resources, ideas, and technology) that have influence on artists today. Create an original piece of art that depicts the subjects, themes, and symbols that demonstrate your knowledge of contexts, values, and aesthetics and that communicate your intended meaning (DOK 4).

» Identify a well-known classical piece of art. Research the historical context within which the piece was created. Identify societal or cultural influences that may have impacted the creation of the piece. Cite evidence from the times to support your interpretations of the influences (DOK 4).

LESSON 6.11
Schools of Art

NCCAS Standards for Visual Arts

» Anchor Standards 1–11

CCSS ELA Standards

» CCRA.R.7
» CCRA.R.9
» CCRA.W.7
» CCRA.W.8

Activities

» Select a time period and research how the studio of a particular artist of the period would have looked. In your project, describe the studio, noting how the equipment might have contributed to this artist's work (DOK 1).

» Research the life of an artist from a historical time period. Determine how his or her personal life may have influenced the art created (DOK 2).

» Create a painting or drawing that incorporates the elements from the school of art we are currently studying (DOK 2).

» Describe how the costumes and lifestyles illustrated in a particular piece of work were faithful to the clothing worn by people in that time period and to the lifestyles they lived (DOK 2).

» While studying a piece of art from a specific "school," develop a mind map describing the feelings you experience from your viewing. Then write a poem or story linked to those feelings (DOK 3).

» Study the politics and economics of the time period reflected in a piece of art from this period. Explain how they are reflected in the piece of art (DOK 3).

» Create a dance, piece of music, poem, or short story that expresses the theme of a particular piece of art (DOK 4).

» In a small group, recreate a painting or sculpture from the style we are studying in a "Living Tableau." This means the group becomes the painting, and holds the pose motionless for 30–60 seconds. The background must be provided by a method of projection (DOK 4).

LESSON 6.12
Study of Art

NCCAS Standards for Visual Arts

>> Anchor Standards 1–11

CCSS ELA Standards

>> CCRA.R.8
>> CCRA.R.9
>> CCRA.W.2
>> CCRA.W.7

Activities

>> Identify a favorite artist and create some work in the style of that artist. Explain how that person's work influenced your own creation (DOK 1).

>> By examining the artists who produced works of art in a particular time period in history, how do you feel their art had been influenced by the economic, social, and political events of that period (DOK 2)?

>> Using visuals, along with published and posted references, demonstrate how the work of a specific artist changed over time. Share your thoughts regarding the reason for the changes (DOK 2).

>> Select two pieces of art to study: one that is classical and the other abstract. Compare and contrast the basic elements of art: line, shape, form, space, texture, and color, including hue, value, and intensity (DOK 3).

>> Locate samples of a famous artist's sketches and then examine that person's later works to compare the sketches to the finished works of art. Describe how they changed and present a personal judgment about the effects of the changes (DOK 3).

>> Investigate the role of female artists over time in one or more movements of art. Use contextual cues to determine whether their paths have seemed more difficult than the paths of their male counterparts in these same areas of endeavor. Provide specific examples and support your conclusions using evidence from the time period, location, artistic endeavor, or other factors (DOK 4).

» Investigate the various careers one could follow that include a significant amount of time with art in some form. Find a person already working in the field and "shadow" that person in person or virtually. Write a log chronicling the experience. Include your observations and your reactions to the events you encounter (DOK 4).

» Compose a work of art that utilizes the elements of art: line, shape, form, space, texture, and color, including hue, value, and intensity of a specific movement or style chosen by the teacher or the student. Provide a context or backstory (DOK 4).

LESSON 6.13
Theatre Arts

NCCAS Standards for Theatre

» Anchor Standards 1–11

CCSS ELA Standards

» CCRA.R.7
» CCRA.R.8
» CCRA.W.2
» CCRA.W.8

Activities

» Examine a program that was distributed to the theatregoers. Locate and explain several passages that help you understand the playwright or cast's efforts to bring the script to life (DOK 1).

» Study the script of a play you have seen performed. Use close reading techniques to locate and read aloud to the group several sections of the script that led to particularly moving scenes in the performance (DOK 2).

» Analyze the similarities between two playwrights who wrote about the same issue in regard to how they tried to "move the audience" to empathy, sympathy, or a better understanding of the characters' actions and behaviors (DOK 3).

» Many plays and other theatrical presentations are based on historical events. Research the background of a specific play that was either specifically or generally about such an event. Research the facts surrounding the event, using primary as well as secondary resources. Then determine the degree to which the portrayal matched the descriptions you have found of the event. Provide rationale to support your decisions (DOK 3).

» To be "literate" in theatre arts means to understand all of its components and goals, although this sometimes depends upon the different theatres and theatre types. Examine position statements from several theatres around the country, including at least one that is in your local community. Offer suggestions as to what the directors might do to improve theatre arts literacy for the young people in their communities (DOK 3).

» Examine the sets and/or the costumes of a play you have viewed. Determine the degree to which they enhanced the messages intended by the playwright. If you judge that some of them were distracting, design some alternatives you believe would have better transmitted the characters' feelings or emotions to the audience. Provide text evidence to support your argument (DOK 3).

» Design a theatre study guide for younger students to accompany a unit of study and a Shakespearean play from a local high school production the students will be viewing. Include a historical perspective, an overall play synopsis, an act or scene-by-scene synopsis, a character breakdown, and critical thinking and reflection questions (DOK 4).

» Locate a play that has been performed pertaining to a certain historical period, such as the Civil Rights Movement or related incidents. Prepare a monologue that could have been read by one of the characters. In your monologue, show what it might have been like to experience the event in the eyes of the character. Include references to the character's emotions and challenging decisions he or she needed to make during this time (DOK 4).

LESSON 6.14
Theatre Arts: Technical Theatre

NCCAS Standards for Theatre

» Anchor Standards 1–3, 5, 9, 11

CSS ELA Standards

» CCRA.R.7
» CCRA.R.8
» CCRA.W.6
» CCRA.W.8

Activities

» Research and explain how the design elements work together in a theatre production. Provide examples of this collaboration (DOK 1).
» Watch a play rehearsal to see what props are needed for a production. Write a props list and draw a sample props table for the play (DOK 2).
» Analyze a play and create a makeup design with a face chart (DOK 2).
» Analyze the play script for technical requirements such as set, lighting, sound. Mark the script and provide notes for recommendation (DOK 3).
» Analyze a play and create a sound design complete with digital music (DOK 3).
» Analyze a play and create a costume design with sketches and fabric swatches (DOK 3).
» Design and create a technical theatre plan that includes: sound board, light board, patch panel, and fly system. Then provide a demonstration to the theatre technical hands and director of the play (DOK 4).
» Create a set design with a ground plan, sketches, and a digital 3D model. Then develop a plan that includes a cost analysis of materials to build the set. Justify both the plans and the cost (DOK 4).

LESSON 6.15

Dance

NCCAS Standards for Dance

» Anchor Standards 1–11

CCSS ELA Standards

» CCRA.R.7
» CCRA.R.8

Activities

» Create a visual that describes the components of three or more types of dance. You may include some you have already performed and/or some you would like to perform (DOK 1).

» Conduct an in-depth study of an accomplished performer in the category of dance you are studying. Include information about her or his challenges and successes. Comment on how his or her experiences influence your own dancing (DOK 2).

» As you observe dance performers in various styles of dance, describe the physical attributes of those people who most likely have had extensive formal training in dance. Include people from several age groups in your study. Report on your findings (DOK 2).

» Examine the dance styles that have appeared for social dancing during three decades that interest you. Create a presentation in which you highlight the connections between events of the times with the type of social dancing that became popular with people in everyday life (DOK 3).

» Focusing on a type of dance your group is currently studying, create and perform an original routine to present to your dance group or other appropriate audience (DOK 3).

» Some forms of dancing, such as tap and ballet, have been popular for many decades or even centuries. Connections have since been made between tap and step dancing, such as that performed by Irish companies. Investigate and report on how dance styles have evolved over time. Draw conclusions based on your findings (DOK 3).

» There has been concern over time about the overall health of professional dancers. Investigate these concerns and create an awareness campaign to bring to your dancing peers so they can be more aware of these dangers and make plans to prevent them (DOK 3).

» Watch several musicals from the 1940s through the 1960s. Identify and share information about the similarities and differences between those presentations and the type of presentations for which you are currently preparing. Consider the impact of societal factors of the time periods being compared (DOK 4).

LESSON 6.16
Fitness

SHAPE America National Standards

- » 1–3, 5

CCSS ELA Standards

- » CCRA.R.7
- » CCRA.R.8
- » CCRA.W.1
- » CCRA.W.2

Activities

- » Record personal data for push-ups, sit-ups, and miles run to monitor your fitness over a period of 1–2 weeks. Be sure the goals you set to improve do not create strain or pain (DOK 1).
- » Locate major muscles that are associated with stretching and warm-ups. Construct a method to impress upon your peers the importance of warm-ups and cool-downs as a regular part of their own exercise program (DOK 2).
- » Boredom is the most consistent enemy of fitness plans. Display methods to reduce or eliminate boredom while working out (DOK 2).
- » With a partner or small group, design an aerobic routine that lasts 3–4 minutes. Describe which muscles are used for each exercise and the benefits derived from the routine (DOK 3).
- » Formulate a game using specific equipment that allows students to compete without compromising their safety (DOK 3).
- » Evaluate your personal fitness level based on norms for your age. Design a program that will improve your level over time. Identify possible challenges that will be faced in reaching your goals and develop ways to overcome these challenges (DOK 3).
- » Design a workout plan that improves the components of muscular endurance, muscular strength, cardiovascular endurance, body composition, nutrition, and flexibility. Provide a statement justifying your choices (DOK 4).
- » Evaluate the effects of aging on fitness and investigate current programs that attend to both factors. Design a better program that addresses these factors (DOK 4).

LESSON 6.17
Physical Education

SHAPE America National Standards

»   1–5

CCSS ELA Standards

»   CCRA.R.7
»   CCRA.R.8
»   CCRA.W.6
»   CCRA.W.7

Activities

»   Study the concept of endurance or strength development. Identify star athletes in several sports who have demonstrated exceptional endurance. Describe the characteristics of endurance in the different sports you identified (DOK 1).

»   Define the concept of agility. Identify star athletes in several sports who have demonstrated exceptional agility. Describe the characteristics of agility in the different sports you identified (DOK 1).

»   Choose a sport in which you have an interest. Gather research about that sport. Include its history, roles, strategies, and famous players. In your project, discuss how the sport has evolved over time (DOK 2).

»   Research the presentation style and methods used by sportscasters in different sports. Identify the characteristics they have in common. Describe or simulate the elements of their individual styles that have made them successful (DOK 2).

»   Write a biographical study of famous outstanding athletes in a designated sport over time. Study people who became stars in their sport and compare and contrast their experiences, skill level, and interaction with the media in their given time period (DOK 3).

»   The physically literate individual exhibits responsible personal and social behavior that demonstrates respect for his- or herself. Examine the choices that students in your peer group may be making that help their physical and mental well-being. Create and post a video addressing the positive decisions people can make persuading others to participate in a healthy lifestyle. Do not use any identifying features (DOK 3).

» Create an exercise and physical activity plan that addresses the needs of your peer group. Design a full body routine that one can do two or three times a week without going to the gym. Incorporate at least 5–10 exercises in your plan that address all of the following areas: cardio, core, push, pull, and quads. Turn in a demonstration video along with your written plan (DOK 4).

» The issues of using anabolic steroids and other illegal body building supplements have long been debated in most organized sports. Investigate reasons why athletes choose to take such substances, the short- and long-term side effects, and create a campaign to increase awareness of this problem (DOK 4).

LESSON 6.18
Creating a Foreign Language Broadcast

World-Readiness Standards for Learning Languages

» 1.1, 1.2, 1.3, 3.2

CCSS ELA Standards

» CCRA.R.7
» CCRA.R.8
» CCRA.W.6

Activities

» Sports report: Report on a recent major event and its results. Include the name of the sport, team, opponent, location played, and final score (DOK 1).

» Weather: Use a map background to convey both your state and your hometown. Incorporate weather phrases, directions (north, south, east, west), and temperatures (DOK 1).

» Write an opening/lead-in: Use music appropriate to the language chosen as a lead-in to the broadcast (or a recording of the school song). Invent call letters or a name for your broadcast. Be creative in the letters you pick. Introduce all your broadcast personalities names along with what they will cover, for example, " . . . et le temps avec Joe Smith!" (DOK 2).

» Report on any big events that are coming soon. Create a brief profile on an outstanding athlete. Include quotes from the athlete and his or her coach (DOK 2).

» Create a news story: Communicate with others in a language of study about the happenings of your school. Use your most important news story as a lead. Suggestions: Think about the "big" events that are going on at your school; don't be afraid to cover issues. Is the school board voting to cut teachers? Did the band win a major competition? Are there any groups doing fundraisers in your school that need a little publicity (e.g., the French club's car wash next Saturday. List where, when, etc.). Begin with a few stories; you may then want to intersperse little news items among the other segments (DOK 3).

» Create a feature report on a topic of timely relevance. Possible ideas include a movie review, an editorial on a local current issue, or a special news report on a national or global occurrence. Cite evidence from which you then draw conclusions for your audience (DOK 3).

» Create a commercial or recreate a popular one of an actual product in the chosen language. Use music and/or props to really "sell" the product. Make connections to your audience to convince them of the need to purchase your product (DOK 3).

» Develop and demonstrate a method for signing off at the end of a newscast. Consider making connections to some of the pressing news stories of the day or synthesizing news items to show a larger context. This may also be an opportunity to include a lighthearted or amusing news item (DOK 4).

LESSON 6.19
World Language

World-Readiness Standards for Learning Languages

» 1.1, 1.2, 1.3, 3.2

CCSS ELA Standards

» CCRA.R.8
» CCRA.R.9
» CCRA.W.1
» CCRA.W.2

Activities

» Explore the contributions made to International Fine Arts by leading artists or musicians from other countries. Report on ways in which these artists have become well-known in the United States (DOK 1).

» Create a Google form to survey your peers to determine if they speak one or more languages, what languages they speak, and how they learned the languages. Also create critical thinking questions posing the advantages of being bilingual (DOK 2).

» Create a picture book for younger students teaching them the basics of the language you are currently studying. Include alpha and numeric lessons, as well as lessons on basic nouns and greetings (DOK 2).

» Locate and interview a person who fluently speaks the language you are currently trying to learn. Conduct and record the interview and provide a transcript in both languages (DOK 2).

» Investigate which languages are most commonly taught in schools in the United States. Collect and display data showing the percentages of languages students study in the United States. Compare these percentages with students living in another country. Draw conclusions and report your findings (DOK 3).

» Investigate a foreign student exchange program available to students at your school. This would include either an English-speaking American who has spent time studying in a foreign country or a student from another country who is now or has in the past visited America in that capacity. Create a multimedia presentation to share the student's experiences with your classmates (DOK 3).

» The guidelines for learning a world language set forth by the American Council of Foreign Language Teachers (http://www.actfl.org) suggest that all world language students should be able to eventually demonstrate:
  ◆ Language control by using the language accurately.
  ◆ Extensive and applicable use of vocabulary in that language.
  ◆ Communication strategies to help maintain communication with another speaker of the target language.
  ◆ Cultural awareness of the people who already speak your target language as their native tongue.

  Assess your level of mastery of these guidelines within the language you are learning, and create a personal education plan of how to obtain these goals (DOK 4).

» Several companies have systems they try to sell to people from one country that would like to become fluent in the language of a different country. Included are Pimsleur, Rosetta Stone, and Fluenz. Each makes advertising claims that their program is the best and easiest to use. Study three of these types of programs. Create a system for rating these companies and explain the reasons for your ratings (DOK 4).

Conclusion

Students have many options to guide their learning. They can choose the types of phones they use, the type of school they attend, and the social media they use. The list is endless, but the point is clear. Teachers can capitalize on students' affinity for choice by building choice into their daily learning. The result? Student engagement, individual challenge, and adherence to the standardized instruction. This system of structured autonomy creates a win-win situation for teachers and students.

Placing the reins of learning into the hands of students promotes true student ownership. These extension lessons provide for active learning that is tailored to address our students' multiple learning levels. Using this semi-structured process ensures differentiated learning experiences that align to the standards while also respecting that students have different interests, different methods of learning, and most importantly, that they are learning at different challenge levels.

Many middle school teachers have had more professional training on teaching specific content and less training on the pedagogy of how to facilitate the teaching and learning of that content. Some may find a challenge in trying to satisfy CCSS expectations without having had sufficient time to prepare for the integration of ELA standards. This book was written with the goal of easing this process.

This book and its contents represent a multiyear effort on our part to assist teachers in providing exciting and highly motivating extension lesson learning activities in all subject areas. With the current expectations that all teachers integrate ELA standards into content rich learning experiences, we knew a resource such as this, that accomplishes that goal of integration, would be welcome with all teachers and students who are in middle or junior high school settings. We hope that you enjoy this novel approach.

References

CongressLink. (n.d.). *Student assessment rubric*. Retrieved from http://teach.oetc.org/files/archives/rubric.pdf

Edutopia. (2012, December 6). *Collaborative learning builds deeper understanding* [Video file]. Retrieved from http://www.edutopia.org/stw-collaborative-learning-math-english-video

Hess, K. (2013). *A guide for using Webb's Depth of Knowledge with Common Core State Standards*. Aberdeen, SD: The Common Core Institute.

Knowles, M. (1975). *Self-directed learning: A guide for learners and teachers*. New York, NY: Cambridge Books.

Mayer, R. E., & Wittrock, R. C. (2006). Problem solving. In P. A. Alexander & P. H. Winne (Eds.), *Handbook of educational psychology* (2nd ed., pp. 287–304). Mahwah, NJ: Erlbaum.

Mursky, C. (2011). *Gifted education in an RtI Framework* [PowerPoint slides]. Retrieved from https://docs.google.com/presentation/d/1NAKeS8rzKqgRkvaw2Bma4X2ixIjXGIi_K8WGuGe0anM/present#slide=id.i0

National Council for the Social Studies. (2013). *The College, Career, and Civic Life (C3) Framework for Social Studies State Standards: Guidance for enhancing the rigor of K–12 civics, economics, geography, and history*. Silver Spring, MD: Author.

National Coalition for Core Arts Standards. (2014). *National Core Arts Standards*. Dover, DE: Author.

National Governors Association Center for Best Practices, & Council of Chief State School Officers. (2010a). *Common Core State Standards for English language arts*. Washington, DC: Author.

National Governors Association Center for Best Practices, & Council of Chief State School Officers. (2010b). *Common Core State Standards for mathematics.* Washington, DC: Author.

The National Standards Collaborative Board. (2015). *World-Readiness Standards for Learning Languages* (4th ed). Alexandria, VA: Author.

NGSS Lead States. (2013). *Next Generation Science Standards: For states, by states.* Washington, DC: The National Academies Press.

Paul, R. (2007 July). *Critical thinking in every domain of knowledge and belief.* Presentation at The 27th Annual International Conference on Critical Thinking, Berkeley, CA.

Peters, S. J., Matthews, M. S., McBee, M. T., & McCoach, D. B. (2014). *Beyond gifted education: Designing and implementing advanced academic programs.* Waco, TX: Prufrock Press.

Reis, S. M., & Renzulli, J. S. (1992). Using curriculum compacting to challenge the above-average. *Educational Leadership, 50*(2), 51–57.

Rollins, K., Mursky, C., Shah-Coltrane, S., & Johnsen, S. (2009). RtI models for gifted children. *Gifted Child Today, 32*(3), 20–30.

SHAPE America. (2013). *National Standards for K–12 Physical Education.* Reston, VA: Author.

Smithson, J. (2004). *Survey of enacted curriculum training material.* Madison: Wisconsin Center for Gifted Education Research, University of Wisconsin.

Strong, R. W., Silver, H. F., & Perini, M. J. (2001). *Teaching what matters most: Standards and strategies for raising student* achievement. Alexandria, VA: ASCD.

Torrance, E. P., & Goff, K. (1990). *Fostering academic creativity in gifted students.* Retrieved from ERIC database. (ED321489)

Washington State University Critical Thinking Project. (2001). *Washington State University critical thinking rubric.* Pullman, WA: The Center for Teaching, Learning, Technology, and General Education Programs, Washington State University.

Winebrenner, S., & Brulles, D. (2012). *Teaching gifted kids in today's classroom: Strategies and techniques every teacher can use* (3rd ed.). Minneapolis, MN: Free Spirit Publishing.

Appendix:
Rubric and Forms

Student Assessment Rubric

Name: _____ Date: _____

	Exemplary 4	Accomplished 3	Developing 2	Beginning 1
Content	Topic standard is exceeded. Substantial pertinent details included.	Topic standard is met. Includes pertinent details.	Working toward standard. Few details included.	Little or no progress toward standard. Few or no details included.
Inquiry skills	Content has been carefully analyzed and evaluated.	Content has been evaluated and analyzed.	Some content has been either evaluated or analyzed.	Little content has been either evaluated or analyzed.
Presentation	Very organized. Uses original approach effectively.	Organized. Uses original approach.	Needs work with its organization. All terms and concepts are not clarified.	Not organized. Terms and concepts are not clarified.
Effort	Consistently on-task throughout the unit. Maintained positive attitude throughout the unit. Met all deadlines.	Regularly on-task throughout the unit. Maintained positive attitude throughout the unit. Met all deadlines.	Usually on-task throughout the unit. Generally had a positive attitude. Met most deadlines.	Rarely on-task. Not always a positive attitude. Often missed deadlines.

Note. Adapted from *Student Assessment Rubric* by CongressLink, n.d., retrieved from http://teach.oetc.org/files/archives/rubric.pdf.

Documentation Forms

A common concern of teachers contemplating having students work on different activities is how to manage the classroom and how to know that students are making progress on their projects. Included here are several forms and checklists that will address this concern and facilitate the process. We recommend reviewing or teaching each element in the lists prior to embarking on their use.

The following documentation forms can be used to:

> help your students manage their time and behavior,

> be respectful of others who are working, and

> provide information and documentation on student progress.

These documents include:

> *How to Work Independently on Extension Activities*: Post these directions in the classroom and/or keep them in students' extension folders.

> *The Essential Rules for Independent Work*: Post this brief list of essential rules— or your version of it—in the classroom as a constant reminder to students.

> *Working Conditions for Extension Activities*: Make this list a classroom chart and/or keep the signed checklist in students' extension folders.

> *Daily Log of Extension Work*: This log can be kept in students' extension folders to document what was planned and what was accomplished each day while working on extension activities.

As you can see, these forms and checklists can be used in a variety of ways: "as is" or modified to meet the needs of the students in your classroom. When starting off, consider discussing and practicing some of the behaviors with your students. Understanding the procedures will ease the transition into this new, independent method of teaching and learning for you and the students.

Note that the Daily Log is at the very heart of successful curriculum differentiation. At the end of each day, students can record what they accomplished and what they hope to accomplish the next day. It gives students practice in learning to set and accomplish realistic short-term goals.

Name: _____ Date: _____

How to Work Independently on Extension Activities

1. Work on your extension activity for the rest of this period.
2. Working with a partner is fine. If you need help, ask your partner for help first.
3. Follow the Essential Rules for independent work at all times.
4. If you need to talk to the teacher, let her or him know (in the agreed upon way) so that you do not interrupt instruction.
5. If you finish early, either begin a new activity or expand upon the one on which you have been working.
6. Complete the Daily Log of extension work.
7. File your extension work in the required location.

Note. Adapted from *Teaching Gifted Kids in Today's Classroom: Strategies and Techniques Every Teacher Can Use* (3rd ed., p. 43) by S. Winebrenner & D. Brulles, 2012, Minneapolis, MN: Free Spirit Publishing. Copyright 2012 by Free Spirit Publishing. Adapted with permission.

Name: _____ Date: _____

The Essential Rules for Independent Work

➤ Work without bothering anyone.
➤ Work on your extension activity without calling attention to yourself in any way.
➤ Refrain from asking the teacher questions while he or she is working with other students.
➤ Complete your selected lesson activity.
➤ Keep records of the tasks you are working on in the way your teacher has explained.

Note. Adapted from *Teaching Gifted Kids in Today's Classroom: Strategies and Techniques Every Teacher Can Use* (3rd ed., p. 44) by S. Winebrenner & D. Brulles, 2012, Minneapolis, MN: Free Spirit Publishing. Copyright 2012 by Free Spirit Publishing. Adapted with permission.

Name: _____ Date: _____

Working Conditions for Extension Activities

Students working on extension activities are expected to follow these guidelines.
1. Stay on task with the extension activity you have chosen.
2. Don't talk to the teacher while he or she is teaching.
3. When you need help and the teacher is busy, ask someone else who is also working on extension activities.
4. If no one else can help you, continuing working on a solution until the teacher is available, or move on to another task until the teacher is free.
5. Use soft voices when talking to each other about the extension activities.
6. Never brag about your opportunities to work on the alternate activities.
7. Don't bother anyone.
8. Don't call attention to yourself.

I agree to these conditions. I understand that if I don't follow them, I may lose the opportunity to continue working on the extension activities and may have to rejoin the class for teacher-directed instruction.

Teacher's Signature: _____

Student's Signature: _____

Note. Adapted from *Teaching Gifted Kids in Today's Classroom: Strategies and Techniques Every Teacher Can Use* (3rd ed., p. 57) by S. Winebrenner & D. Brulles, 2012, Minneapolis, MN: Free Spirit Publishing. Copyright 2012 by Free Spirit Publishing. Adapted with permission.

Daily Log of Extension Work

Student's Name: _____

Project Topic: _____

Today's date	What I plan to do during today's work period	What I accomplished today

Note. Adapted from *Teaching Gifted Kids in Today's Classroom: Strategies and Techniques Every Teacher Can Use* (3rd ed., p. 92) by S. Winebrenner & D. Brulles, 2012, Minneapolis, MN: Free Spirit Publishing. Copyright 2012 by Free Spirit Publishing. Adapted with permission.

About the Authors

Dina Brulles, Ph.D., is the Director of Gifted Education at Paradise Valley Unified School District, Gifted Program Coordinator at Arizona State University, and serves on the NAGC Board of Directors. Dina coauthored *The Cluster Grouping Handbook, Teaching Gifted Kids in Today's Classroom*, and *Helping All Gifted Children Learn*.

Karen Brown is the Gifted Program Mentor for Paradise Valley Unified School District. Mrs. Brown consults with districts on curriculum mapping, Common Core curriculum implementation, and differentiation strategies. She works extensively with teachers to ensure that the instruction and curriculum provides the appropriate challenge and support for all students.

Susan Winebrenner, M.S., is the author of *Teaching Kids With Learning Difficulties in Today's Classroom, The Cluster Grouping Handbook*, and *Teaching Gifted Kids in Today's Classroom*. Susan is currently a full-time consultant in staff development specializing in highly practical and effective training for educators in differentiated instruction.

Common Core State Standards

This book aligns with an extensive number of the Common Core State Standards. Please visit http://www.prufrock.com/ccss to download a complete packet of the standards that align with each extension lesson this book.